Across the Curriculum

with Favorite Authors

Donald Crews/Ann Jonas

written by Cynthia Holzschuher

Illustrated by Agi Palinay

Teacher Created Materials, Inc.
P.O. Box 1040
Huntington Beach, CA   92647
©1995 Teacher Created Materials, Inc.
Made in U.S.A.

ISBN-1-55734-456-6

Table of Contents

Sample Plan—Crews/Jonas

This basic plan is presented in three sections to help you organize and simplify the presentation of the books in this volume. It serves well as a general guide and may be adjusted and adapted to specific titles.

Before the reading . . .

❑ Ask the students to share their feelings and experiences with the topic.

Examples:

Do they have a favorite blanket?

Do they have baby siblings?

Have they ever ridden a train, boat, or plane?

❑ Give them something to look or listen for.

Examples:

Look for Donald Crews in the illustrations.

Look for the ways Mr. Crews shows movement.

Look for visual games in Ms. Jonas' work.

❑ If possible, share tangible items related to the topic.

Examples:

quilt	flashlight
bicycle helmet	mirror
tote bag of toys	

During the reading . . .

❑ At appropriate intervals, stop and ask comprehension questions.

Examples:

Do you have a racing bike?

What do you see on your walk to school?

❑ Ask other questions requiring critical thinking.

Examples:

What if the mother bear had left the cubs?

What is the best form of transportation? Why?

❑ Stop and predict what will happen on the next page.

Examples:

When the train is getting closer, what will happen next?

When Deborah rings the doorbell, what will happen next?

After the reading . . .

❑ Complete some or all of the suggested activity sheets, games, and crafts.

❑ Assign the homework pages where appropriate.

Donald Crews

Donald Crews was born August 30, 1938, in Newark, New Jersey. He is a free-lance artist, writer, and photographer. He is married to Ann Jonas, who is also a free-lance artist and writer. They have two daughters, Nina and Amy. The family lives in Brooklyn, New York.

Donald Crews designed his first children's book, *We Read: A to Z*, while in the army and stationed in Germany. He has written and illustrated many children's books, including two Caldecott Honor Books—*Freight Train* (1979) and *Truck* (1980). His story books *Bigmama's* (1991) and *Shortcut* (1992) tell about his childhood when he rode the train to visit his grandparents in Florida. Donald Crews believes that children should explore many art forms as a positive way to express themselves.

You may wish to write to him at the following address:

Greenwillow Books
105 Madison Avenue
New York, NY 10016

Donald Crews—Bulletin Board

Enlarge the train patterns on page 30 to fit across your bulletin board. You will need an engine, a caboose, and five cars. Cut them from brightly colored construction paper. On each car, print one of these letters: R-E-A-D-I-N-G. Attach the train to the middle of the board. Draw a prominent track underneath the train.

Cut letters for these words:

Bicycle Race

Summary

The 12 cyclists in this book change positions as they race to the finish line. One racer's bicycle needs repair but he manages, with extra effort, to come back and complete the race.

Activities

❑ Distribute the pattern on page 8. Assign the children numbers and colors for their racers and combine them in groups of 12 to use in number books.

❑ Use the pattern on page 8 for a matching activity for colors and color words. Color the racers as you wish. Make color word cards for matching.

❑ Make the same activity for numbers and number words. Another time, show a group of several bicycles in numerical order, leaving out one or more numbers. Ask students to identify the missing numbers.

❑ Look for Donald Crews among the race spectators. He is wearing a yellow shirt.

❑ Have students complete the activity sheet on page 9. Have them add the wheels with paper fasteners and draw themselves as the riders. Ask them to write a story describing their bikes or explaining why they enjoy riding.

❑ Discuss the antonyms associated with the race: start/finish, win/lose, stop/go, fast/slow, front/back. Have students use each pair of antonyms in sentences unrelated to bicycles.

    Example:
- I usually win when I play checkers.
- I sometimes lose when I play bingo.

❑ Brainstorm a list of bicycle safety rules.

Bicycle Race *(cont.)*

Activities *(cont.)*

❑ Make a yes/no graph for the answers to these questions:

- Do you have a bicycle? (yes/no)
- Do you wear a helmet when you ride your bike? (yes/no)

❑ Organize a footrace on the school track. Give the racers numbers and discuss how the participants may have changed positions during the race.

❑ Prepare the game board on page 10.

❑ Challenge your students to make a replica of a book bicycle from long, colored pipe cleaners.

Creative Writing Questions and Topics

❑ How do you think number nine felt when her bicycle broke down?

❑ What would you have done? Do you admire her extra effort?

❑ Would you like to participate in a bicycle race? What would be good about it? What would be bad?

❑ Who lost the race? How can you tell? How would it feel to lose? How would you react if you were the loser?

Bibliography

BMX Freestyle by Larry Brimner (Watts Publishing, New York, 1987)

Let's Visit a Bicycle Factory by George Ochoa (Troll Associates, New York, 1990)

Wheels! The Kids' Bicycle Book by Megan Stine (Little, Brown, New York, 1990)

Bike Rider

Activity Sheet 1: Use this pattern to design a rider for the class book of numbers.

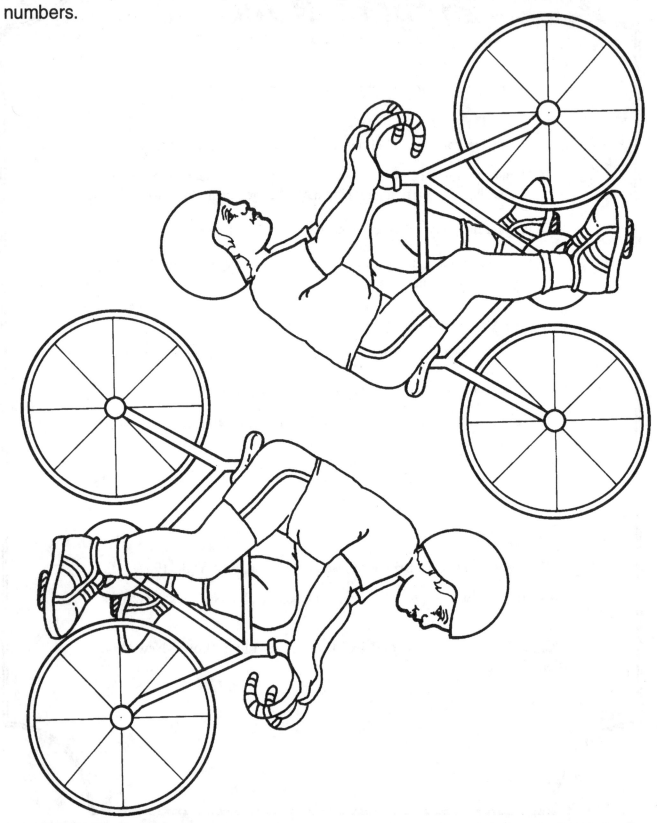

My Bike

Activity Sheet 2: Cut off the wheels and attach them to the bicycle with paper fasteners. Draw yourself on the bike. Write a story about why you like to ride your bike.

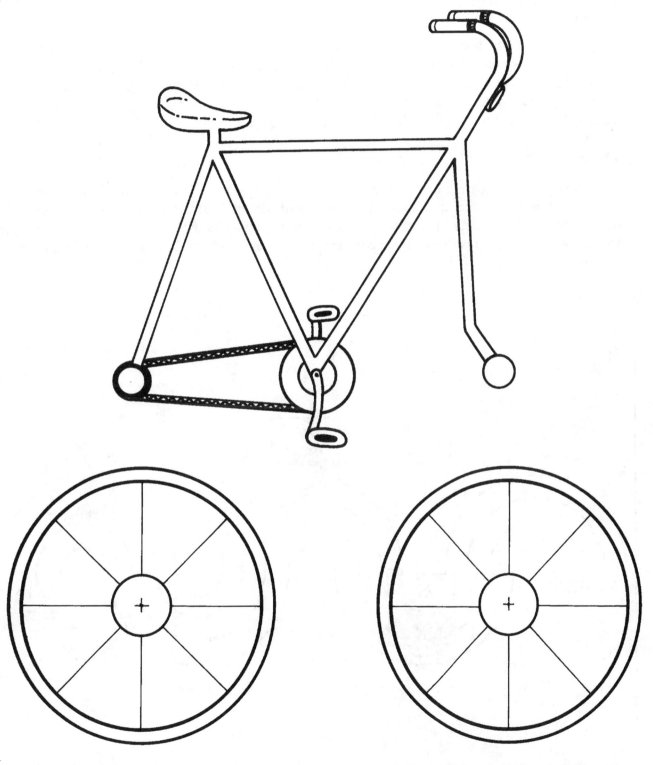

Game Board

This game board can be used for any questions addressed in the study of bicycles. Safety, number words, color words, antonyms, or comprehension questions about bicycle building and racing would all be appropriate topics.

To Make:

You will need four copies of the semicircle. Cut them apart and assemble as the race path (see diagram). Mark two sections with START and FINISH signs. You may wish to mount the path between two sheets of clear contact paper for stability, or leave it unassembled for easier storage. Color and cut the racers. Mount on tagboard and make them freestanding in small balls of clay. Color the remaining bicycle and use paper fasteners to insert the spinners.

To Play:

All racers begin at the starting line. Players may use either spinner. They spin and move along the race path as they correctly answer questions. All players will continue moving forward unless some player's spin stops in the red section of the spinner. At that point, all players will move backwards for one turn. Play resumes, moving forward (until someone spins red again), and the first racer to the finish line is the winner.

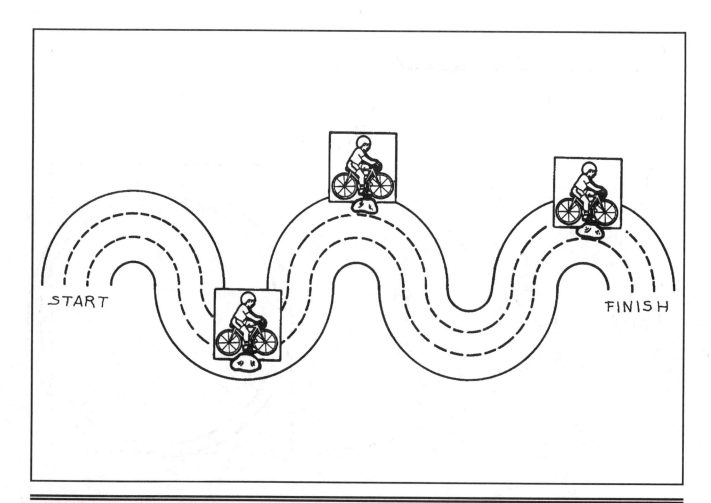

Bicycle Game

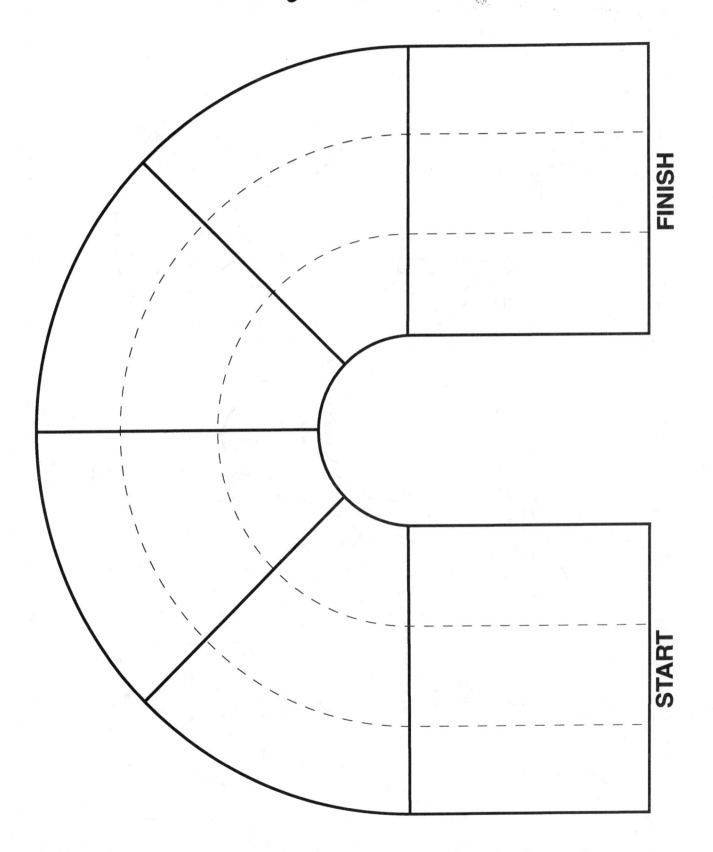

FINISH

START

Bicycle Game (cont.)

Playing Pieces

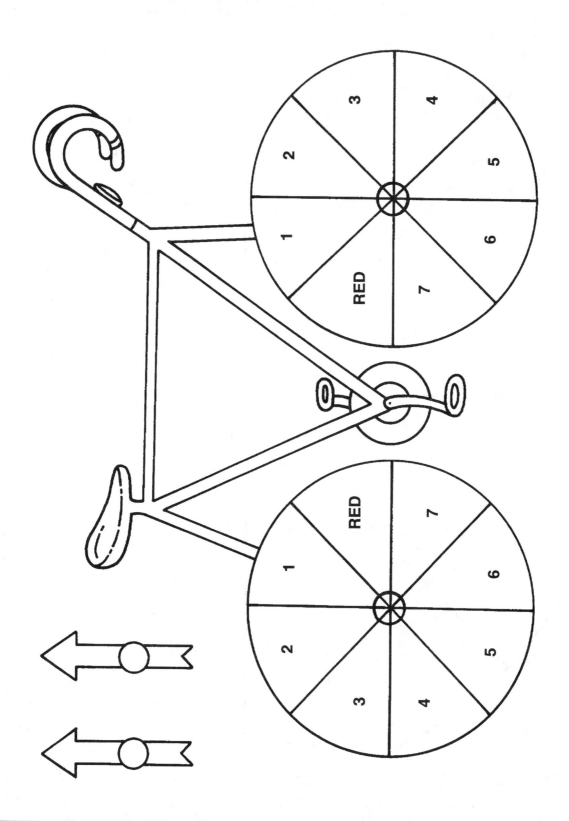

Bigmama's

Summary

The author remembers his childhood trips with his family to spend the summer at his grandparents' home in Florida. Their farm offers many happy experiences and memories for the author, his brother, and two sisters.

Activities

- ❏ On a map, locate Newark, New Jersey, (Donald Crew's boyhood home) and Cottondale, Florida (his grandparents' home where he spent the summer).

- ❏ Have students use the activity sheet on page 15 to complete their family trees. Remind them to include aunts, uncles, and cousins.

- ❏ This book gives a clear picture of the farm surroundings and outbuildings. Use the information in the book to make an aerial map of these locations. Remember to include details from the illustrations in the book.

- ❏ Extend the experience of *Bigmama's* by having students write original stories about events that might have taken place during the summer on the farm. These may be about horseback riding, fishing, or the animals. Combine the stories into a class book. Read *Shortcut* by Donald Crews (Greenwillow Books, 1992) to learn of one true life adventure.

- ❏ Use the house on page 16 as a shape book cover. For the inside pages, ask students to draw the family dinner and write a story with information about the experience.

Bigmama's *(cont.)*

Activities *(cont.)*

❑ The train trip takes three days and two nights. Ask students what kinds of things they think children might do with that much time on a train. Enlarge the train car pattern on page 30 to use as a shape book cover. Ask students to draw pictures inside the book of the family (two boys, two girls) and their activities during the trip.

❑ Have students complete the diary on page 17 with information about what they will do for three days and two nights.

❑ Ask what kinds of things they would pack for a summer vacation in Florida. Have students complete the activity sheet on page 18 by filling the suitcase with things they will need for the trip.

❑ Discuss with the students the differences between city and country life depicted in this book (well water, outhouse, animals, fishing, etc.). If appropriate, have students complete a Venn diagram comparing the two settings.

Creative Writing Questions and Topics

❑ Tell what you might do with your next summer.

❑ Have you ever taken a train trip? Tell about the experience.

❑ Would you prefer city or country life? Why?

❑ How do you travel to visit your grandparents? Tell about your most recent trip.

Bibliography

Train by John Coiley (Dorling Kindersley Books, 1992)

Shortcut by Donald Crews (Greenwillow Books, New York, 1992)

The Train to Grandma's by Ivan Gantschev (Picture Book Studio, 1987)

Family Tree

Activity Sheet 1: Complete this family tree with the names of people in your family. Write the name and birth date of one family member on each leaf. Ask a parent for help with filling in birth dates. Cut the leaves out and glue them on the tree. Color the tree. Use blank leaves for other relatives such as brothers, sisters, aunts, uncles, and cousins.

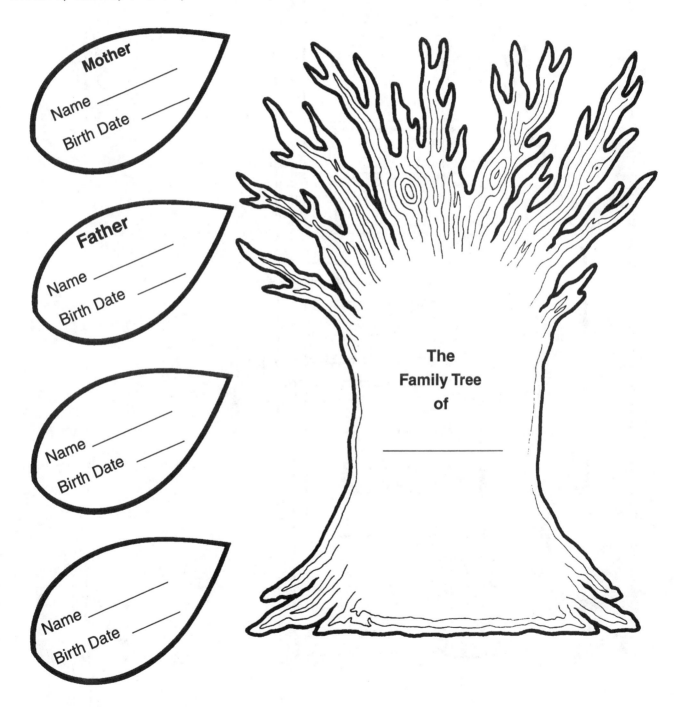

Mother
Name _____
Birth Date _____

Father
Name _____
Birth Date _____

Name _____
Birth Date _____

Name _____
Birth Date _____

The
Family Tree
of
_____

House Pattern

Activity Sheet 2: Color and cut out this house to use as a book cover. Write a story and make a picture of your family having a big dinner.

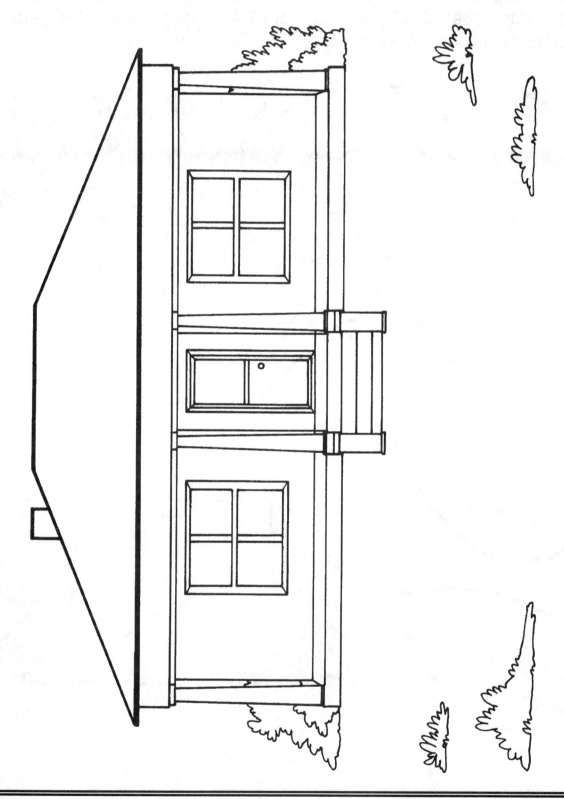

Daily Diary

Activity Sheet 3: Fill in this diary page with information about what you have done for three days and two nights.

Summer Suitcase

Activity Sheet 4: In this suitcase, draw the things you would pack for a summer vacation in Florida.

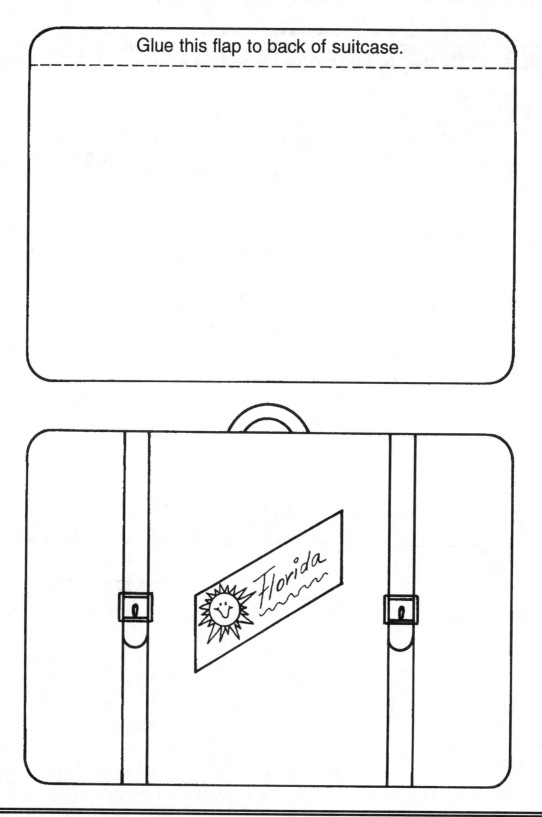

Glue this flap to back of suitcase.

Carousel

Summary

The text and illustrations in this book depict the movement of a carousel ride.

Activities

❑ After sharing the book, let the children model the movement of the carousel ride by rolling their hands in front of them or tapping a table in a slow-fast-slow pattern. Remind them that the pattern simulates the slow start and finish of the ride.

❑ Discuss the antonyms *up/down, fast/slow,* and *stop/go.* Ask the students to say or write sentences indicating how these words relate to the carousel ride.

❑ Look at the dedication in this book: To MAMANNINAMY (to Mama, 'n Nina, Amy). Donald Crews has dedicated this book to his wife (Ann Jonas) and daughters, Nina and Amy.

❑ Have students design a carousel of their own. This carousel may be made by a group of three to six students. They will need the following materials:

- 12 cardboard tubes from toilet paper (6" or 15 cm)
- 6 cardboard tubes from paper towels (12" or 30 cm)
- 1 cardboard tube from gift wrap (20–24" or 50–60 cm)
- 2 cardboard circles (20" or 50 cm in diameter)
- aluminum foil
- crepe paper streamers
- curling ribbon (optional)
- a sheet of colored tissue paper (optional)
- six carousel horses (colored and cut out)
- scissors, adhesive tape, stapler, hole punch (optional)

Carousel *(cont.)*

Activities *(cont.)*

Teacher Preparation: Split the 12 short tubes lengthwise and tape them together again so that their new diameter is about one inch narrower. Make several small cuts around the ends of each short tube and fold them out so that they can stand upright. Arrange six tubes around the perimeter of each cardboard circle. Staple and tape them firmly in place. Be sure that the spacing is the same on both circles. These will be the top and bottom of the carousel.

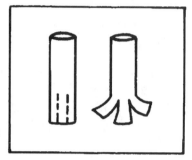

Student Preparation: Each student should wrap his 12-inch (30 cm) tube with aluminum foil and tape it in place. Punch a hole in the top of each tube and tie on a few lengths of curling ribbon. Tape or staple the prepared horse on both sides of the tube. When all six horses are on their poles, stand them on the prepared carousel bottom.

Carefully add the top, inserting the short tubes inside the horse poles. Cover the tall gift-wrap tube with aluminum foil and insert it through a hole in the center of the top. Add a flag of colored tissue paper and more curling ribbon for decoration. To finish, cut lengths of crepe paper streamers, tape them firmly to the top center pole, twirl them, and staple them at each horse on the top cardboard circle.

If available, set your carousel on a lazy Susan base so that it can spin.

❑ If you do not wish to make the entire carousel, have students make a horse on a pole with ribbons to take home.

Carousel *(cont.)*

Activities *(cont.)*

❑ Listen to "The Carousel Waltz" from *Carousel* by Rodgers and Hammerstein, Original Cast (Decca MCA).

❑ If possible, take a walk to a playground that has a merry-go-round.

❑ Have students finish the activity sheet on page 22 by coloring the horse and adding the color words.

❑ Have students design another amusement park ride or draw a picture of another ride that they have enjoyed. How is it like/not like a carousel?

Creative Writing Questions and Topics

❑ Tell about a time when you rode a carousel. Include your feelings about the experience (sights and sounds).

❑ Where is there a carousel near your home? What other things do you associate with amusement parks, fairs, carnivals, etc.? (food, clowns, other rides)

Bibliography

Up and Down on the Merry-Go-Round by Bill Martin, Jr., and John Archambault (Henry Holt, 1988)

The Merry-Go-Round by Kathryn Shoemaker (Holiday House, 1985)

Merry-Go-Rounds by Art Thomas (Carolrhoda Books, Minneapolis, 1981)

Happy Horse Pattern

Activity Sheet 1: Color and cut out this horse for your carousel pole.

Spinning Carousel

To make a spinning carousel you will need the following:
- a one-pound (500 g) coffee can with the top and bottom removed
- two plastic lids to fit the top and bottom of the coffee can
- an 18" (45 cm) dowel stick (1" or 2.5 cm diameter)
- two copies of the carousel activity sheet
- glue, scissors, markers, and art supplies to decorate the can

What to Do:

Color the activity sheet as you wish. If supplies are available, decorate it with glitter, sequins, yarn, etc. Cut out the carousel pattern and glue it to the outside of the coffee can. Cut a small X in the center of both plastic lids. Put the lids on the can. Insert the dowel stick carefully through the top and bottom. If you wish, add curling ribbon and a flag to the top of the pole. Make the carousel spin by holding the pole at the top and rubbing it back and forth between your hands. It may be necessary to add masking tape under the bottom lid to keep the can from slipping down.

Spinning Horses

Activity Sheet 2: Use this page for your spinning carousel. Color and cut it out.
Glue it to the coffee can. Use two copies to cover the whole can.

Flying

Summary

This book allows the reader to take part in an airplane flight from takeoff to landing over all kinds of scenery and terrain.

Activities

❑ Copy the pattern (page 27) onto construction paper or lightweight tagboard. Have children color, cut, and assemble the plane.

❑ Assign several children to draw scenes from the book (runway, airport, highway, river, city, country, mountains) on a large sheet of butcher paper. They may use their airplanes on the scenery to retell the story.

❑ On another day the students may use their airplanes to demonstrate positional concepts—over/under, above/below, etc.—in the scenery.

❑ Have children work in groups to make sequenced books of the plane ride. They should draw only the scenery, not the airplane. There will be 10 pages from takeoff to landing back at the airport. Assemble the pages in order and staple into book form. Make a small airplane and staple it to a craft stick. On each page of the book, cut a slot (with a craft knife) where the airplane would be. Children may insert the airplane into the slots as they "read" the book.

❑ If possible, arrange a visit to an airport near your school. If it is a major airport, look for people working at jobs other than those of pilots and flight attendants.

❑ Have the students research the careers of pilot and flight attendant.

Flying *(cont.)*

Activities *(cont.)*

❑ Have students practice folding several different styles of airplanes from paper. Have contests to see which will fly the farthest or come closest to hitting a specific mark.

❑ In the book illustrations, have students look for a passenger who looks like Donald Crews.

❑ If appropriate, contact airlines to find the cost of some commuter flights to cities near you. Compare the costs on a chart. Mark the destinations on a map.

Creative Writing Questions and Topics

❑ If you have ever flown on a plane, write about your experience. What did you like or dislike?

❑ What are some reasons people might take an airplane trip?

❑ How are helicopters used where you live?

Bibliography

Tomorrow, Up and Away by Pat Lowery (Collins, Houghton, 1990)

Planes, What's Inside? by (Dorling Kindersley, 1992)

Paper Plane Pattern

Activity Sheet 1: Color and cut out this airplane. Fold on the dotted lines. Ask your teacher to cut the slots for the wings and tailpiece.

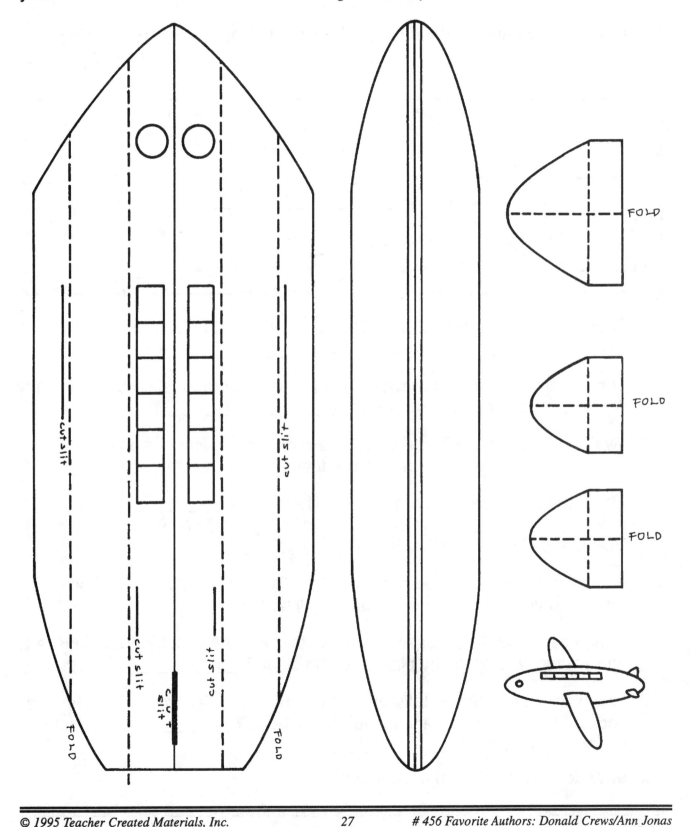

Airplane Arithmetic

Activity Sheet 2: Use the planes from Activity Sheet 1 to demonstrate these word problems.

You may make a hangar for the planes from a large box turned upside down. Cut a large half-circle opening in one side for a door. Create a runway with tape lines on the floor.

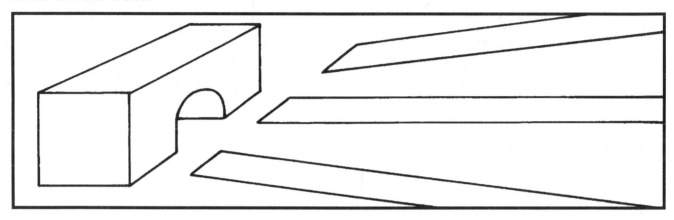

1. Four planes are on the runway. One plane is about to land. How many planes in all will soon be on the ground?_____

2. Three planes are on the runway. One plane is about to take off. How many planes will be left on the runway?_____

3. Two planes are in the hangar. Three are on the runway and one plane is about to land. How many planes are there in all at this airport?_____

4. The planes are parked at the airport. There are _____ planes in row 1, _____ planes in row 2, and _____ planes in row 3. How many planes are there in all? _____

5. There are 8 planes parked at the airport. Two planes are taxiing down the runway to take off. How many planes will be left?_____

6. A man can clean three airplanes every day. He will work Monday, Tuesday, and Thursday. How many planes will he clean? _____

7. Five planes are ready to take off. One plane has a flat tire and one has an engine problem. How many planes can take off? _____ How many must be fixed? _____

Extra: Write a word problem of your own.

Freight Train

Summary

The reader follows a train as it moves through tunnels, across trestles, and past cities, in darkness and daylight.

Activities

❑ Use the patterns on page 30 to make a color train. You will need one engine, six cars, and one caboose. Print "black" on the engine and "red" on the caboose. On the six cars print these color words: orange, yellow, green, blue, purple, and brown. Color the cars correctly. Cut them out and glue together. Display your train on the bulletin board.

❑ Use the patterns on page 30 to make a number train. You will need one engine, 10 cars, and one caboose. Cut out the cars and glue them to a large piece of paper. When your train is complete, number the cars 1–10 and draw people in them to equal the numbers. Display your train on the bulletin board.

❑ You may prepare the activity above for use at a center by cutting the train pieces from colored tagboard, numbering them, and punching holes in the front and back of each one. Provide enough paper fasteners for your students to join the cars in sequence. With a fine-point permanent marker, draw "smiley" faces on 55 plastic chips to be used as people when counting the sets to each car.

❑ Cut a random number of the train patterns (page 30) in several colors for sorting and graphing by color and shape. Younger children may use the cars for counting and patterning activities.

❑ Have students complete the word search puzzle on page 31 about train vocabulary.

❑ Have students compare train and airplane travel on a Venn diagram.

❑ Have students look for the initials N and A on the train engine. They refer to Donald Crews' daughters, Nina and Amy.

Creative Writing Questions and Topics

❑ Why do you think some people like to travel by train rather than airplane?

❑ Watch for a train passing near your home. What do you think it is carrying?

Bibliography

Thomas, the Tank Engine by W. Awdry (Heinemann, 1990)

Thomas the Tank Engine and Friends by W. Awdry (Random House, 1992)

The Freight Train Book by Jack Pierce (Carolrhoda Books, 1980)

Friendly Freight Pattern

Activity Sheet 1: Cut out the patterns below and follow your teacher's directions.

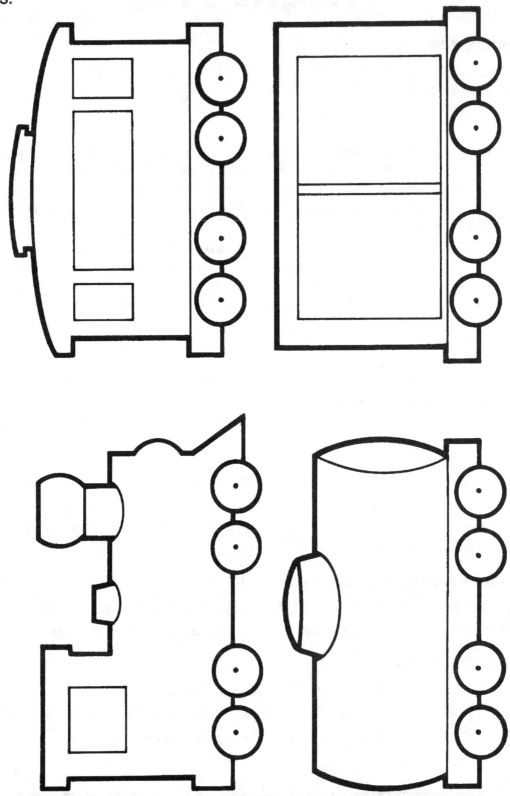

Word Search

Activity Sheet 2: Find the train vocabulary in this word puzzle.

train	caboose	smoke
tunnel	freight	city
track	engine	trestle

```
E A B T R A C K
N T C U D E A F
G H S N N Y B G
I G M N I T O H
N I O E A I O I
E E K L R C S J
T R E S T L E K
R F W P O N M L
```

Harbor

Summary

This book introduces the young reader to the various kinds of boats that travel through a busy harbor.

Activities

❑ Contact a travel agency for information about cruises. Ask them to provide brochures showing the interiors of cruise ships and the activities available. Mark the departure points and destinations on a map.

❑ Have the class look carefully at a map of the United States. Mark several major harbors like New York, Boston, San Francisco Bay, etc.

❑ Contact a recruiter near you for information about the Navy and Coast Guard.

❑ Have students make a book showing the different "ship shapes" as pictured on the last page. Label each one.

❑ Prepare this simple science experiment. You will need the following:

- recycled foam coffee cups with lids
- straws
- paper for sails
- scissors and stapler
- a small amount of gravel or sand
- a tub of water or a water table

Make a boat by putting the lid on the cup and inserting the straw like a mast. Design a sail on paper, cut it out, and staple it to the mast. Make another boat the same way but include some sand or gravel in the cup to act as ballast. Ask the children to predict which boat will sail better. Use your hands to make waves and watch what happens!

Harbor (cont.)

Activities (cont.)

❑ Have students use the activity sheet on page 35 to design a boat of their choice. Notice the tugboats are named after Donald Crews' daughters, Nina and Amy.

❑ If you have a large enough surface of water, your students will be able to try steering a barge. You will need the following:

- two or three small foam meat trays
- one foam coffee cup
- one small plastic margarine dish
- some twist ties
- a hole punch and stapler
- a straw
- paper for a flag
- sand or gravel for ballast

Put some sand or gravel in the margarine dish. Turn the coffee cup bottom up and stand it in the dish to create a tugboat wheelhouse. Design a small flag and staple it to the straw. Make a hole and insert it in the side of the cup. Use the hole punch and twist ties to connect the two foam trays to each other and the "tugboat." Experiment using the tug to push the barges in the water. Try it again with some weight (erasers, paper clips, etc.) on the barges. Record what happens.

Creative Writing Questions and Topics

❑ Have you ever been on a boat? Tell about your experience.

❑ Do you think you would enjoy life as a sailor? In what ways?

❑ Interview someone who has been on a cruise. Would this person recommend it to a friend?

Bibliography

Sailboat Lost by Leonard Everett Fisher (Macmillan, 1991)
Boat Book by Gail Gibbons (Holiday House, 1983)
Big City Port by Betsy Maestro (Four Winds Press, 1983)
The Wreck of the Zephyr by Chris Van Allsburg (Houghton Mifflin, 1983)

Boats, Boats, Boats

Activity Sheet 1: Cut out the pictures below and glue them next to the correct sentences.

Ferryboats carry cars back and forth from shore to shore.	
Tugboats push and pull big boats to their docks.	
Fireboats are ready to take care of emergencies or celebrations.	
Barges are loaded with sand and gravel.	

My Boat

Activity Sheet 2: Design the boat that you would like to own.

Light

Summary

With simple drawings, the author presents various types of light, natural and artificial, in city and country settings.

Activities

❏ Have students research information about Thomas Alva Edison. Make a list of some of his inventions other than the light bulb. Complete the activity sheet on page 38.

❏ Brainstorm a list of things that people used for light before electricity, (candles, gaslights, oil lamps). Ask students what they use for light at their houses when the electricity goes out during a storm. (flashlight, candles)

❏ As a class, make a list of words that describe light (bright, shiny, twinkling, etc.). Use those words in sentences to show their meanings.

❏ Ask your students to bring in flashlights. Use colored plastic wrap (blue, pink, and green) to make filters. Shine the prepared flashlights on colored items or pictures. Ask students to predict what will happen when the items are illuminated with colored light.

❏ Provide several cereal boxes and sheets of recycled foil (or gift wrap) to make this city at night scene. Open one end of the box and turn it inside out. Look at the pictures from the book and design similar buildings from the boxes. Cut holes for the windows. Glue foil sheets behind the windows. Tape the boxes shut and stand them together. Make a night sky of dark blue paper with foil stick-on stars. Darken the room and shine a flashlight "moon" on your scene. Make a similar country scene if desired.

Light (cont.)

Activities (cont.)

❑ Remind the children to notice the movement of the sun in the sky during the school day. Discuss where the sun rises and sets and mark east and west points in your classroom.

❑ Brainstorm a list of things that have (or give) light. Illustrate each one for a class book. Glue foil to the items to make the lights "shine."

❑ Have students design suns from yellow paper plates (like the one in the book) and sprinkle them with gold glitter. Hang them from the ceiling.

❑ Share the poem "Shadow Race" from *A Light in the Attic* by Shel Silverstein. Take the children outside on a sunny day at noon and again later in the afternoon. Measure the length of their shadows each time and compare the difference. Discuss how the length of shadows will change as the sun is lower in the sky.

❑ Share these poems about natural light: "Night Comes . . ." by Beatrice Schenk de Regniers and "Song" by Ruth Krauss; both are from *The Random House Book of Poetry for Children,* 1983.

Creative Writing Questions and Topics

❑ How do you feel when alone in the dark?

❑ How would your life be different if there were no electricity?

❑ Which do you prefer, day or night? Why?

Bibliography

Light and Sound by Melvin L. Alexenberg (Prentice Hall, 1969)

Light and Color by Louis Wilmer Anderson (Raintree Books, 1988)

Exploring Light by Ed Catherall (Steck Vaughn, 1990)

House Lights

Activity Sheet 1: Draw four things that give light at your house. Bring this paper back to school to share with the class.

The Light Bulb

Activity Sheet 2: Read this story. Answer the questions.

Thomas Alva Edison

Thomas Edison was born in Milan, Ohio, February 11, 1847. He went to school for only three months. After that his mother taught him at home. When he was a teenager, a train accident left him deaf. Thomas Edison loved to do scientific experiments and often worked 18 hours a day in his laboratory. He invented many things, but he is best remembered for the electric light bulb.

1. Where was Thomas Edison born? _____

2. When was he born? _____

3. Why did he become deaf? _____

4. What did he enjoy doing? _____

5. How long did he work some days? _____

6. What is his most important invention? _____

Bonus: Read about Thomas Edison in an encyclopedia and make a list of his other inventions.

Parade

Summary

In this brief story, the author presents the sequence of activities that takes place on parade day. The vendors, spectators, and participants assemble for an exciting and colorful event.

Activities

❑ Have students look at the various elements of the parade (marching band, food vendors, floats, etc.) and discuss them in terms of the senses to which they appeal. Sort them on a list with three categories: sight, sound, and taste.

❑ Have the class research the flags in the parade. List the countries from which they come and make similar flags (stapled to drinking straws) to use in a class parade or to "sell" like a street vendor.

❑ Ask students to look for Donald Crews among the old-fashioned bicycle riders in the parade.

❑ Listen to recording(s) of march music like *I Love a Parade*, CBS Records (John T. Williams) or *Stars and Stripes Forever, Sousa Marches*/Vanguard Records (University of Michigan Band). Have the children choose an instrument to play in a pantomimed parade.

❑ As a class, determine a theme (fairy tales, Mother Goose, etc.) for a parade of floats made of shoe boxes. In small groups, allow students to work at designing an appropriate entry. Have the groups write or tell about the process and share it with the class. Display all the floats in parade formation for classroom visitors to see and enjoy.

Parade *(cont.)*

Activities *(cont.)*

❑ If possible, invite high school band members to visit your classroom with their instruments and uniforms. Ask them questions about performing in a marching band; compare their instruments and uniforms to the ones pictured in the book.

❑ Use the patterns on page 43 to make a math activity. Color, cut out, and mount the vendors on tagboard. Assign each item a price and allow students to practice counting money necessary for "purchases." They may count coins to pay for an item or subtract the price from a given amount of money. This activity may be extended to multiplication if students select and pay for several of the same item.

❑ If possible, share a video of a holiday parade taped from television. Discuss the visual impact and why so many people seem to love parades.

Creative Writing Questions and Topics

❑ Have you ever been in a parade? Tell about your experience.

❑ If there was a parade in your town today, would you want to see it? Why? Why not?

❑ Look back at the parade participants in this book. Which one would you like to be? Why?

Bibliography

The Parade Book by Ed Emberley (Little, Brown, New York, 1962)

Crash! Bang! Boom! by Peter Spier (Doubleday, New York, 1972)

Parade by Harriet Ziefert (Bantam Books, New York, 1990)

Parade Mural

❑ Allow children to work in small groups to design a parade mural. Assign each group a specific parade unit to draw. Except for the spectators, each group should be drawn together on a separate panel. The spectators can be drawn in variously sized groups and cut apart. Use the patterns on page 44 to get started.

- marching band
- baton twirlers
- vehicles
- flag corps
- floats
- spectators

❑ Another group of students may be in charge of writing (or improvising) a script or dialogue for the parade. When all the components are complete, decide on a parade order and tape them together. Make sure the dialogue is in correct sequence and present your parade to another class.

Parade Patterns

Activity Sheet 1: Use these patterns to make a math activity. You will need these patterns and some coins.

Parade Patterns *(cont.)*

Activity Sheet 2: Use these patterns to help complete the parade mural. (You may wish to enlarge the patterns.)

School Bus

Summary

Several school buses leave the parking lot and move across the city to pick up children for school. When school is over, they retrace their paths to return the students to their homes.

Activities

❑ Ask students to look for Donald Crews in the illustrations.

❑ Rewrite the text in sentences. Read or tell the new version.

❑ Invite a school bus driver to visit your classroom. Ask questions about the schedule, route, and training. What (if anything) must the bus driver do to maintain the bus?

❑ Brainstorm a list of bus safety rules. Make illustrations and display each one on a separate poster.

❑ Make a graph showing how your students get to school.

❑ Sing "The Wheels on the Bus." Discuss the antonyms that apply to buses. Brainstorm a more complete list of antonyms. Write sentences to show their meanings.

❑ Have students compare and contrast a ride on a school bus and city bus. If appropriate, take your class on a short city bus trip.

❑ Choose one bus that is used by your students. Mark the route on a map. Add the time the bus arrives at each stop. From that information, print a bus schedule. Practice reading other schedules (bus, TV, movies, etc.).

Creative Writing Questions and Topics

❑ Would you like this book better if the people had faces?

❑ What happens (what do you see) on your bus trip to school?

❑ Describe your bus driver.

❑ If I were school bus driver, I would . . .

Bibliography

Bus Riders by Sharon Denslow (Maxwell Macmillan, 1993)

What's It Like to Be a Bus Driver? by Judith Bauer Stamper (Troll Associates, 1990)

Bus Patterns

Activity Sheet 1: Cut out the door, windows, and wheels. Attach the wheels with paper fasteners and the windows and door with glue. Draw children in the windows. Print your school name on the side of the bus.

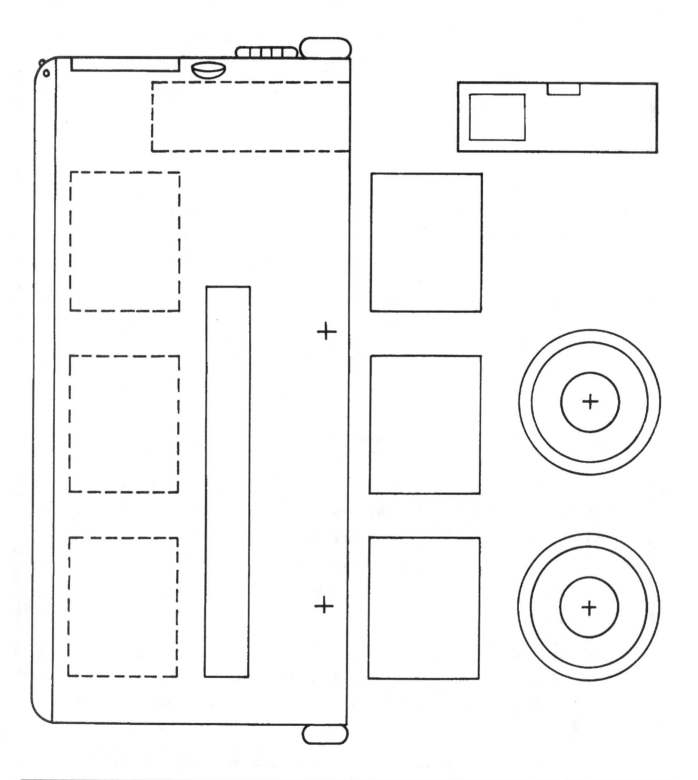

Bus Patterns (cont.)

Activity Sheet 2: Cut apart the children at the bottom of the page. Seat them in the bus to show math facts from your teacher.

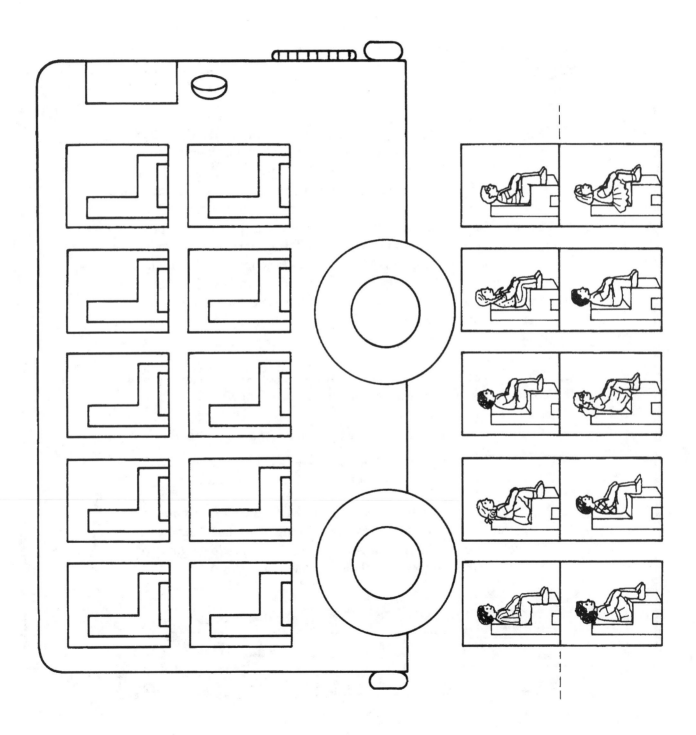

Shortcut

Summary

In this true story from the author's childhood, seven friends walk home along a railroad track and find that taking the shortcut can be exciting and dangerous.

Activities

❏ Work with the students to create an ensemble of vocal train sounds. You may use the words from the book, ("klakity klak" and the whistle "whoo") and add others like "choo-choo," "toot-toot," and "chugga-chugga." Divide the group into sections, assign the repeated rhythmic patterns, and, if desired, plan a way to write down the parts. The ensemble should be performed as if the train is approaching, passing, and leaving (the same as in the story). The children should understand the soft-loud-soft progression of sounds. Practice with one child as "conductor." You may wish to use a sandblock to keep a steady beat. If available, a cowbell can add interest to the accompaniment. If you wish, the conductor may experiment with changing speed as well as volume.

❏ This is a true story from Donald Crews' childhood. Discuss or write about events in your life that may have been dangerous.

❏ As a group, compare and contrast passenger trains and freight trains.

❏ Learn to sing "Down by the Station" (*Wee Sing Children's Songs and Fingerplays*). Share the poems "Train Song" by Diane Siebert and "Travel" by Edna St. Vincent Millay (*The Random House Book of Poetry for Children*, Random House, New York, 1983)

Shortcut *(cont.)*

Activities *(cont.)*

❑ Take a walk around your neighborhood to look for railroad tracks and signs. Discuss with the class safety practices for railroad tracks. Have the students draw pictures of the railroad signs and the crossings near your school. If there are several, show them on a simple map.

❑ Have the class role play what the children might have said if they had told Bigmama about their experience that night.

❑ Enlarge the train patterns on page 30 to make an accordion fold book. Each car will be a page. The students may illustrate the approach, passing, and departure of the train on the individual cars or write their ideas of how the children must have felt that night as the train passed.

❑ Have the students complete the activity sheet on page 50 with information from the story.

Creative Writing Questions and Topics

❑ How do you think this experience changed the children's behavior with regard to trains?

❑ What kinds of things make you afraid? When you feel afraid, what can you do to make yourself feel better?

❑ Did the children make a good decision to follow the railroad track that night? What should they have done?

Bibliography

Train Whistles by Helen Sattler (Lothrop, Lee, Shepard Books, 1985)

Train Song by Diane Siebert (Crowell, 1981)

Track, Train, and Home

Activity Sheet 1: Draw a train with four cars on the railroad track.

❏ Draw seven children walking on the track.

❏ Make an X on the spot where you think the children jumped off the track.

❏ Draw a line to show the path they took home after the train passed.

❏ Draw Bigmama's house at the end of the road.

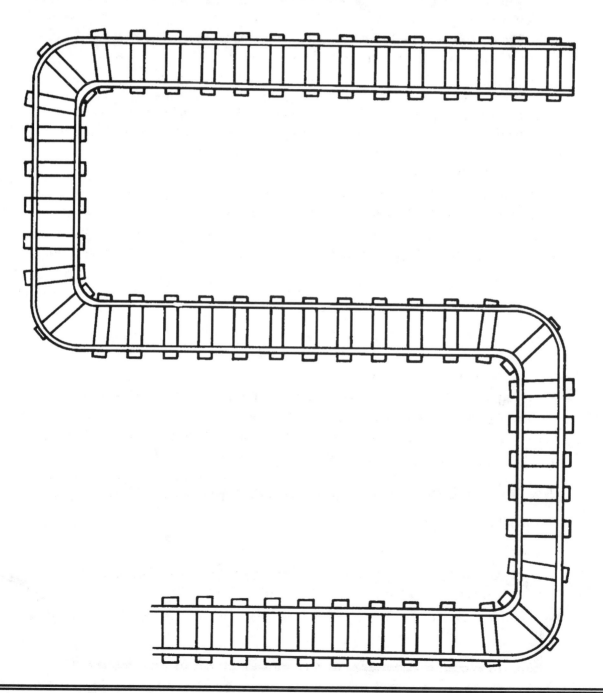

Ten Black Dots

Summary

This counting book explores what can be done with ten black dots in graphic art and rhyming text.

Activities

❑ Cut numerals 1–10 from colored tagboard. Make a corresponding number of holes in each numeral with a hole punch. Lay these numerals over black construction paper so that the black dots are apparent. The young student may practice counting sets by placing plastic counting chips over the holes.

❑ Cut several rectangles (3"x 6" or 7.5 cm x 15 cm) from heavy white paper. Divide them in half to represent dominoes. Use a hole punch to make a total of 10 holes in each one. (Each domino should show a different combination of sets.) Lay the prepared dominoes over black paper so that the dots are apparent. The student will determine the numeral for each side by counting the dots and then will write an addition fact with the sum of 10. Use this activity with the activity sheet on page 52.

❑ Use the activity sheet on page 53 to make a matching game. The students may match numeral to word, numeral to set, word to set, or all three (numeral to word to set).

❑ Read the book carefully and make a list of the rhyming words. Brainstorm additional words from the same rhyming families or words that rhyme with each number word (one-fun, two-blue, three-see).

❑ Encourage children to look for circles in other items around the classroom. Have them picture the things they find and indicate the number of circles with a numeral or word.

❑ Make a class book titled *What Can You Do with Ten Black Dots?* Ask children to picture things in the environment that have circles (or dots). If possible, write or dictate a rhyming couplet for each picture.

❑ Have students learn to recite or sing counting rhymes and songs like "One, Two, Buckle My Shoe" and "This Old Man."

❑ Allow each student to cut his/her own set of 10 black dots from paper. Students may use the dots for outlining letters (as well as numbers).

❑ Provide several other counting books (see bibliography) in a center. Encourage children to design their own theme-related counting books or illustrate one of the counting rhymes or songs.

Bibliography

Each Orange Had Eight Slices: A Counting Book by Paul Giganti, Jr., illustrated by Donald Crews (Greenwillow Books, 1992)

Anno's Counting Book by Mitsumasa Anno (Thomas Y. Crowell, 1975)

Lots of Dots

Activity Sheet 1:

- Make 10 dots on each domino.
- Count the dots on each side.
- Fill in the blanks to write the addition facts.
- Be sure the sum is always 10.

Example:

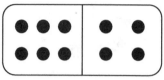

_6_ + _4_ = _10_

Double Your Dots

Activity Sheet 2 (Teacher's Note): Cut apart the cards to make a matching game. According to which you wish to emphasize, select either word cards or figure cards to go with the dots. Have student partners turn the cards over and take turns trying to make a match. Continue until all the cards have been matched. The player with the most pairs at the end is the winner.

●	one	1
● ●	two	2
● ● ●	three	3
● ● ● ●	four	4
● ● ● ● ●	five	5
● ● ● ● ● ●	six	6
● ● ● ● ● ●	seven	7
● ● ● ● ● ●	eight	8
● ● ● ● ● ● ● ● ●	nine	9
● ● ● ● ● ● ● ● ● ●	ten	10

Truck

Summary

A truck hauls a load of bicycles through highway traffic and bad weather to arrive on time at its destination.

Activities

❑ Trucks are used to carry many things. Ask students to think about the different kinds of trucks that they see every day. Choose one of them to make from the pattern on page 56. Have them color the cab and write a story about that truck on the trailer. Cut another trailer and draw a picture of what is inside the truck. Cut a third trailer to design as the outside of the truck. It will be the cover of a book. Staple all the trailers together at the top to make a shape book.

❑ Discuss the things that are brought to your area by truck. Give each child a copy of the truck (page 56) to design as they wish. Cut out the trucks and tape them along a baseboard in the reading area of your classroom. Label the display "Keep on Truckin'."

❑ Cut a large truck from tagboard, laminate it, and cut it apart to use as a puzzle.

❑ Ask the students to look for street (traffic) signs as they travel to and from school. Draw them and share with the class to learn the meanings.

❑ Make a concentration-style matching game from pairs of the most important signs.

❑ As a group, dictate words for the story of this book. On another day, write the story of the truck as it returns.

Truck *(cont.)*

Activities *(cont.)*

❑ Have students complete the activity sheet on page 57 to encourage them to be aware of trucks around them.

❑ Discuss the weather conditions pictured in the book. How is weather a problem when driving a truck?

❑ Ask your students to bring their toy trucks to class. Count the wheels, sort, and graph them accordingly.

❑ Discuss the similarities and differences between 18-wheelers and pickup trucks.

Creative Writing Questions and Topics

❑ Have you ever ridden in a truck of any kind? Where did you go? How was it different from a car ride?

❑ Would you like to be a trucker? Why? Why not?

Bibliography

The Neighborhood Trucker by Louise Borden (Scholastic, 1990)

Trucks by Stephen Oliver (Alladin Books, 1991)

Wheels by Venice Shone (Scholastic Books, 1990)

Galimoto by Karen Lynn Williams (Mulberry Books, 1990)

Truck Pattern

Activity Sheet 1: Follow your teacher's directions for the pattern below.

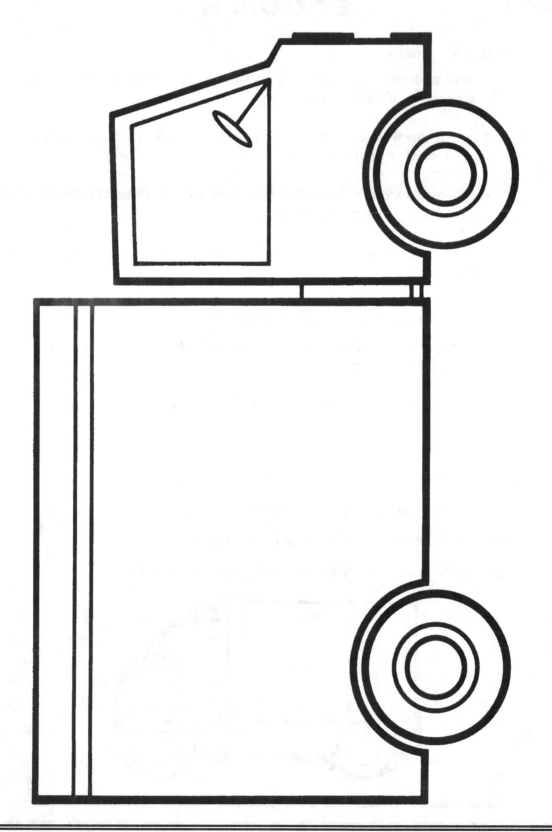

Truck Homework

Activity Sheet 2: On this form, list some information about the trucks you see around town. You may ask an adult to help you.

	Name on Truck	State License Plate	What Is It Hauling?
1.			
2.			
3.			
4.			
5.			
6.			

U·R·SPCL

We Read: A to Z

Summary

This is Donald Crews' first book, written as an addition to his portfolio while he was still in the army. The book introduces all 26 letters as well as showing numerals 1–26. It also teaches positional concepts through language and graphic art.

Activities

- ❏ Have students work in small groups to act out the concepts, using only their bodies.

- ❏ Brainstorm an ABC list of foods, animals, or proper names.

- ❏ Make available a set of letters to be arranged in ABC order.

- ❏ Sing "The Alphabet Song" to the tune of "Twinkle, Twinkle Little Star."

- ❏ Have children position themselves like specific letters or ask groups of children to elect a leader who will arrange all of them into a single letter shape.

- ❏ Read other alphabet books and use them as models to make your own. Children may work in groups to select themes for their books.

- ❏ Draw pictures to show an understanding of these concepts: **few/many, inside/outside, top/bottom, over/under,** and **vertical/horizontal.** Use only the colors red, orange, yellow, blue, green, and black to make your illustrations similar to the book.

- ❏ Have students use alphabet-shaped cereal to spell their names or other words that they know.

- ❏ Have students make a collage of letters showing different newspaper fonts.

We Read: A to Z *(cont.)*

Activities *(cont.)*

❑ Have students look for initials used commonly in daily life (U.S.A., etc.).

❑ Cut large tagboard letters and decorate them with the same letter cut from newspapers or catalog pictures beginning with that initial consonant.

❑ Play the following word game: You will need a set of alphabet cards. The students should stand in two lines. Show the letter card. Each student (alternating teams) should say a word that begins with that letter. Play continues until a player cannot think of a word. He is out and must sit down.

❑ Have students print their initials. Include them in a picture that has something to do with themselves, their friends, or school.

❑ Make several sets of these shapes from laminated construction paper.

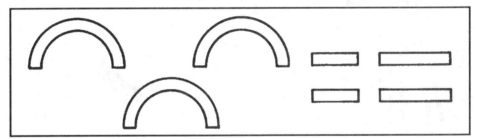

❑ Distribute a set to each student or group of students to use in forming letters.

Bibliography

Eye Spy by Linda Bourke (Chronicle Books, 1991)

Alphabet Out Loud by Ruth Bragg (Picture Book Studio, 1991)

The Letter Book by Ivan Bullock (Simon and Schuster, 1991)

Jambo Means Hello by Muriel L. Feelings (Dial Press, 1974)

A to Zen by Ruth Wells (Picture Book Studio, 1992)

Hidden Letters

Activity Sheet 1: Find the hidden letters in this picture. Trace over them with a black crayon. Color the rest of the picture.

Complete This Picture

Activity Sheet 2: Finish the letters to read the message. Draw yourself in the picture.

Alphabetical Order

Activity Sheet 3: Fill in the letter to show what comes before, between, and after.

A B C _____   L M _____ O P

_____ E F G   F G H _____

S T _____ V W   _____ R S T

M N O _____   J K _____ M N

_____ O P Q   W X Y _____

❏ ❏ ❏ ❏ ❏ ❏ ❏ ❏ ❏

Put these letters in ABC order.

S T R V U   ____ ____ ____ ____ ____

P R Q O S   ____ ____ ____ ____ ____

D B A C E   ____ ____ ____ ____ ____

Ann Jonas

Ann Jonas was born January 28, 1932, in Flushing, New York. She graduated from Cooper Union Art School and has worked as a graphic artist for many years with her husband, Donald Crews. She lived in Germany for 18 months when her husband was in the army. Their first daughter, Nina, was born there.

She has written four American Library Association Notable Books: *The Quilt* (1984), *Holes and Peeks* (1984), *The Trek* (1985) and *Round Trip* (1983). Her book *Round Trip* was also named one of *The New York Times* Best Illustrated Children's Books (1983). Many of her books contain "visual games" that involve the reader. She says of her books, "I try to play visual games against the background of a believable situation, to involve the child on an emotional level as well. The prime purpose of the book should be to entertain, but if it can reassure the child a bit in the process, that's even better." She uses the photographs her husband has taken of their family over the years to help her remember what kids actually do.

Ms. Jonas lives in Brooklyn, New York, with her husband and two daughters, Nina and Amy. You may wish to write to her at the following address:

> Greenwillow Books
> 105 Madison Avenue
> New York, NY 10016

Ann Jonas—Bulletin Board

Distribute the quilt square pattern (page 79) to each student. Have students design either a square representing a book title or a flowered square. Cut the squares and glue them to a large sheet of paper to resemble a quilt. Add crayon "stitches" and, if desired, a pretty border. Cut two sets of letters for the words "Look at a Book," and one set of letters to spell "by Ann Jonas." Attach the quilt to the bulletin board. Above the quilt staple a piece of aluminum foil. Arrange the letters as shown in the diagram below.

Aardvarks, Disembark!

Summary

After the flood, Noah calls out a group of little-known, often endangered or extinct animals. At the end of this book, there is brief reference information about each animal.

Activities

❏ Learn more about the story of Noah and the flood. Have children work in groups to make dioramas that picture different scenes from the story. You will need to provide each group with art supplies and a small, sturdy box.

❏ Have students research information on one of the animals from this book. Next, have them present a short report to the class or make a poster with a large picture and a list of the facts they learned.

❏ Ask students to choose one of the animals, look carefully at the picture, and write a descriptive paragraph about the animal's appearance.

❏ Have the class make lists that classify these animals by characteristics—horns, beaks, number of toes or legs, etc.

❏ Brainstorm an alphabetical list of animals commonly seen in zoos. Choose 10 animals from this book and put those names in ABC order.

❏ Make an ark-shaped book. On each page, have students picture a pair of animals of their choice, along with a short story about them. For younger children, make a large ark (front and back) that lifts open at the top. Ask children to make pictures of animals in pairs to glue inside the ark.

❏ Let the class look at pictures of an assortment of animals. Describe how they are the same or different. Sort them into groups and be prepared to explain the basis for the classification.

❏ Check with your local zoo to see if they display any of the animals in this book. Visit the zoo if possible and have students write about their impressions of favorite animals.

❏ Share the books, *Hey! Get Off Our Train* by John Burningham, Crown Publishers, 1989, and *The Great Kapok Tree* by Lynne Cherry, Gulliver Books, 1990, to learn more about endangered animals and habitat destruction. Be sure that children understand the meaning (and seriousness) of extinction.

Creative Writing Questions and Topics

❏ What do you think it would be like to live through a flood?

❏ What would have happened to the animals without the ark?

❏ What is the difference between an endangered animal and an extinct one?

Bibliography

From Albatross to Zoo by Patricia Borlenghi (Scholastic, 1992)

A Children's Zoo by Tana Hoban (Greenwillow Books, 1985)

Wild Animals of America ABC by Hope Ryder (Lodester, 1988)

From Rare to Extinct

Activity Sheet 1: Classify these animals as rare, endangered, or extinct. Use the information at the back of the book to help you.

lemur	tamarin	marabou	uakari
yak	jacana	wallaby	dodo
capybara	eland	aurochs	aardvark
addax	tarpan	wapiti	hartebeest
quagga	shoebill		

	Rare	Endangered	Extinct
1			
2			
3			
4			
5			
6			
7			
8			
9			
10			

Creatures and Clues

Activity Sheet 2: Read the clues. Match the creatures. Glue in place.

1. This field mouse is found all over the world. (vole)	
2. This bird from Africa is related to storks and herons.	
3. This animal is a relative of the giraffe.	
4. This is a small Australian kangaroo.	
5. This is a large constricting snake from South America.	

Bonus: Write two clues of your own and draw the animals.

Pairs and Partners

(Teacher's note: You will need two copies of this page to make the game.)

Activity Sheet 3: Noah took animals in pairs onto the ark. Play this game with a friend to match the animal pairs. Cut apart the pictures, turn them over, and take turns finding the pairs.

Color Dance

Summary

Four dancers use scarves to show color mixing. At the end, there is factual information about the occurrence of colors on the color wheel.

Activities

❑ Provide small amounts of tempera or finger paints for children to explore color mixing.

❑ Have students look through a large box of crayons and classify them by their primary colors. Another time, arrange them into a color wheel similar to the one at the back of this book. Learn the names of unusual colors. Why are they named as they are?

❑ Ask each child to make a story about his/her favorite color. Combine them into a class book about colors.

❑ Distribute one page each of different colors of construction paper. Ask children to cut clothing from catalogs to match the color of their paper and combine the pages in a book called Color Catalog.

❑ Have students do research to learn what it means to be color blind.

❑ Distribute colored crepe-paper streamers. Ask the children to move to the ballet music of Tchaikovsky.

❑ Let students look at an item of clothing that is multicolored. Identify all the colors, using the learned vocabulary (from crayons).

❑ Play the game Riddle-ee Ree for color identification skill.

"Riddle-ee, riddle-ee, riddle-ee Ree,

I see something that you don't see, and it is (color)."

Creative Writing Questions and Topics:

❑ How do colors make you feel?

❑ Write about colors that make you feel happy, sad, tired, etc.

❑ Have you ever taken dance lessons? Tell about your experience.

Bibliography

Is It Red? Is It Yellow? Is It Blue? by Tana Hoban (Greenwillow, 1978)

A Color Sampler by Kathleen Westray (Ticknor and Fields, 1993)

Colors by Phillip Yenamine (Delacorte Press, 1991)

Household Hues

Activity Sheet 1: Take this sheet home. Name things at your house that are these colors.

1. pink   _____   _____

2. green   _____   _____

3. orange   _____   _____

4. white   _____   _____

5. brown   _____   _____

6. purple   _____   _____

7. blue   _____   _____

8. yellow   _____   _____

9. red   _____   _____

10. black   _____   _____

Food Color Wheel

Activity Sheet 2:
Read the color words and color the wheel.

Think of a fruit or vegetable for each color.

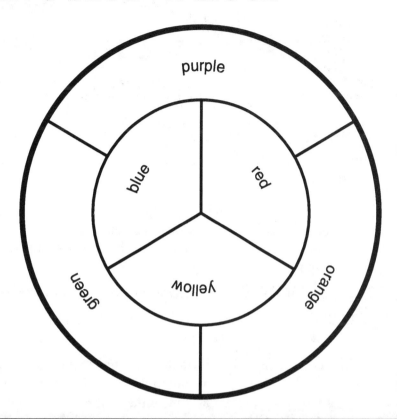

	Color	Fruit	Vegetable
1	green		
2	orange		
3	red		
4	blue		
5	yellow		
6	purple		

Holes and Peeks

Summary

A little boy does not like holes unless they can be fixed or plugged, but peeks are fun because he can see things through them.

Activities

- ❑ Provide children with magnifying glasses and binoculars and encourage them to peek at interesting things in the classroom. If desired, you may bring a collection of items which have details that are improved with magnification.

- ❑ Ask students to look for Donald Crews' red truck among the boy's toys.

- ❑ Take a walk or search the classroom for holes. These may be in clothing, a sink, a sewer, snake holes, etc.

- ❑ Make a class book of riddles with hints about things that have holes or peeks. Cover each picture (answer) with a flap. Use a hole punch to make a few holes in the flap so that the answer is almost evident.

- ❑ Have students complete the homework activity sheet on page 73. Ask them to look around their houses or yards for holes.

- ❑ Have students complete the activity sheet on page 74. Help them learn other words that begin with *H* or *P*.

- ❑ Decorate a shoe box and cut a hole in one end big enough for a child's hand to fit through. Place something in the box and have the children take turns trying to identify it by touch only.

Creative Writing Questions and Topics

- ❑ How do you feel if a favorite toy or item of clothing is damaged or gets a hole in it?

- ❑ Write a language experience story about one hole shown in the book.

- ❑ What would happen if there was a hole in your pocket? In your shoe? In your sock?

Bibliography

Hide-and-Seek by Susanna Gretz (Macmillan, New York, 1986)

I Won't Be Afraid by Joan Hanson (Carolrhoda, Minnesota, 1972)

Holes at Home

Activity Sheet 1: Use this paper to draw four pictures of holes you found at your house or in your yard.

Extra: Bring something from home that has a hole or a peek to share with the class.

H and P

Activity Sheet 2: Cut out the word cards at the bottom of this page. Glue them near the correct pictures.

Vocabulary

H	hat	hand	house	heart	horn	horse
P	pencil	plane	puzzle	paint	paper	puppy

Now We Can Go

Summary

A child is not ready to go until she transfers all the toys from her toy box into a large red tote bag.

Activities

- ❑ Each child will need a sheet of red construction paper. Cut one-inch (2.5 cm) strips from the long side. Fold the paper in half and glue the strip to one end as a handle. This is the red tote bag from the story. Ask the children to draw the little girl's toys (or their own toys) on white paper, cut them out, and glue them inside the bag. Children may share the contents of their "bags" for a language activity or write a story about the toys if appropriate.

- ❑ Brainstorm a list of the class toys from the tote-bag activity.

- ❑ Use the pictures from the activity sheet on page 77 to make flannel board pieces. You will also need a blue toy box and a red tote bag. The children may move the pieces from the box to the bag in sequence with the book and have experience with the concepts less/more and full/empty.

- ❑ Have students complete the activity sheet on page 77. Label the toys and number them in the order they were shown in the book.

- ❑ Use the pictures on page 77 to make a graph showing the toys your students have at home.

Now We Can Go *(cont.)*

Activities *(cont.)*

❏ Homework: Look around your room and draw pictures of six things that you might pack for a trip to Grandma's house. On the other side of your paper, draw six things you would take to visit a friend overnight. How are the two sides alike/different?

❏ Make a take-home story kit similar to the flannel board activity. Students each make a blue box and a red bag from construction paper and then color and cut out a set of the toy pictures (page 77). They may use this with the book to make "reading" more concrete.

❏ Discuss various means of transportation and try to decide how the little girl will be traveling. Allow each child to express an opinion and chart the responses on a graph.

❏ Have students look for the cover of this book among the little girl's toys.

Creative Writing Questions and Topics

❏ Sequence another set of common activities, like waking up in the morning through arriving at school.

❏ Where do you think the little girl is going? Why?

❏ What will she do when she arrives?

Bibliography

How to Travel with Grownups by Elizabeth Bridgman (Crowell, 1980)

On the Road by Sally Kilroy (Viking Press, 1986)

Toy Sequence

Activity Sheet 1: Print the names of these toys under their pictures. Number them in the order they appear in the story.

There are nine toys in the book.

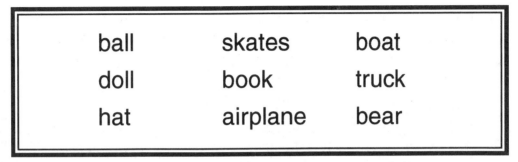

ball	skates	boat
doll	book	truck
hat	airplane	bear

The Quilt

Summary

In this story, a little girl dreams of an adventure stitched into her new patchwork quilt.

Activities

- ❑ Individually or as a group, have the students write a story of the little girl's dream. Where did she go looking for Sally? Draw a map of her dream.
- ❑ Make a class book of favorite stuffed toys. This may be in the shape of Sally, the little girl's blue dog. The text should include the description and name of each toy.
- ❑ Let the class look at a book of traditional quilt patterns. Have them use the activity sheet on page 79 to reproduce some of the individual favorites. Label them for a display.
- ❑ Have the students use the activity sheet on page 79 to design a quilt square about the story. Cut out the squares and glue them (like a quilt) to a large sheet of paper. Add "stitches" (crayon marks) between the squares. If possible, print a summary of the story around the border.
- ❑ Homework: Use the activity sheet on page 79 to reproduce a square from a family quilt. Share the pictures with the group.
- ❑ Toward the end of the year, have the students use the pattern to make a quilt of class memories. Cut the squares and glue them to a large paper backing. In a center square, print the room number and year.
- ❑ For young children, use the square pattern to make an ABC or number quilt.
- ❑ Have the students use the activity sheet on page 80 to make their own quilts. It must have a repeated design and color pattern.

Creative Writing Questions and Topics

- ❑ Write about a dream you have had or would like to have.
- ❑ Write about your favorite stuffed toy.
- ❑ Have you ever been to a circus? Tell about the experience.
- ❑ Draw a picture and write a story about your bedroom.

Bibliography

The Patchwork Quilt by Valerie Flournoy (Dial Books, 1985)

The Quilt Story by Tony Johnston (Putnam, 1985)

The Keeping Quilt by Patricia Polacco (Simon and Schuster, 1988)

Quilt Pattern

Activity Sheet 1: Use this pattern for activities about quilts.

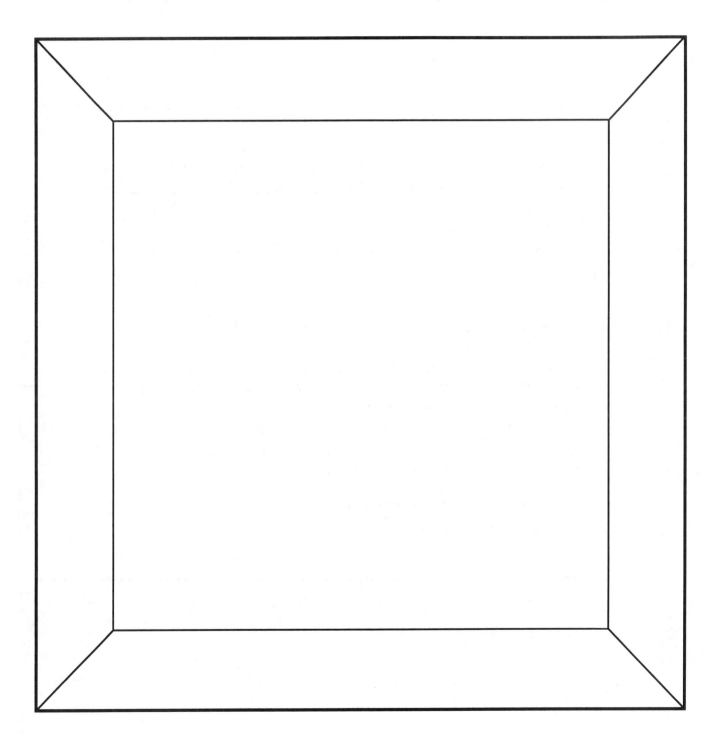

Quilt Pattern *(cont.)*

Activity Sheet 2: Make your own quilt. It must have a repeated design and color pattern.

Reflections

Summary

The book traces a child's day with visits to the beach, carnival, campground, and woods. When the book is turned upside down, a second picture is reflected in each original.

Activities

❏ Make a panel big book with sentence strips that sequence the activities of your school day. Have children work in groups to produce books. They will need to include all the subjects and events of the day with illustrations. Accordion-fold the panels and staple at the left.

❏ Ask students to choose a partner and stand facing each other for this mirroring activity. Either child may be the leader with the other following his/her movements. Encourage the pairs to explore an interesting variety of movements.

❏ Distribute paper and crayons or markers and challenge students to make a drawing that could have meaning when turned upside down.

❏ Have students keep a daily journal with a mirror of foil decorating the cover. All the information should be written in the same first-person style as the story.

❏ Use a map to locate 10 beaches in the United States. Make a chart to show which of these your students may have visited.

❏ Cut out the letters R-E-F-L-E-C-T-I-O-N-S. Invite students to arrange these letters to spell smaller words.

❏ Have students make pictures and write stories about a rain storm that may have occurred recently in their area.

❏ Brainstorm lists comparing things to do on land and water.

❏ Ask students which of the pictures in this book is their favorite. Why?

❏ Reread the story. Have the students try to determine a verb that describes the action on each page. Make a list of the verbs. They all should have an -ing ending (fishing, walking, eating, flying, etc.).

Creative Writing Questions and Topics

❏ What is the best place you know? Why?

❏ Would you have enjoyed the day described in this book?

❏ Describe the weather conditions at the beach.

❏ Have you ever gotten up at dawn? What is that like?

Bibliography

Making Faces by Nick Butterworth (Candlewick Press, 1993)

Exploring Light by Ed Catherall (Steck Vaughn, 1990)

Shadows and Reflections by Tana Hoban (Greenwillow Books, 1990)

Sailboat Story

Activity Sheet 1: Use this paper for a story about a day on the water—swimming, sailing, or fishing. Color the bottom of the boat, cut it out, and fold on the dotted lines.

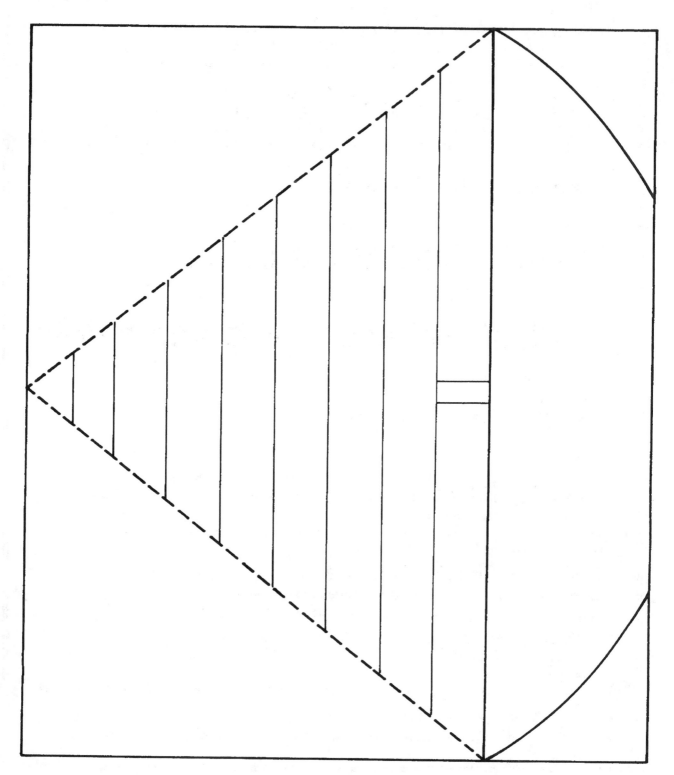

Story Sequence Strips

Activity Sheet 2: Cut apart these strips and glue them on another piece of paper in order to tell the story.

I wake up at dawn.

I watch the men fishing.

I go to the beach.

I catch a frog at the pond.

I walk in the woods and see a deer.

I feed the ducks.

I go to bed.

I go to a carnival.

I eat dinner.

I fly a kite.

Round Trip

Summary

A family wakens early in the morning for a car trip from their country town to the city. When the visit is over, the reader turns the book around to complete the journey home.

Activities

❑ Ask students to choose two contrasting colors of construction paper. They should draw a picture outline similar to one in the book and cut it from one piece of the paper. Glue the outline squarely to the top of the contrasting color. Turn the paper over and glue the other cut half at the bottom.

❑ Make a reversible city/country book. Design two covers, one showing a city scene and one showing the country. Have students work together to write stories about city/country life. Staple the story pages to their corresponding covers, so that they have two books without back covers. Reverse one of the books (to become the back cover) and staple them together at the left.

❑ Let students look at the art of M. C. Escher. It is in black and white and is similar to the illusions in this book.

❑ Have students complete a Venn diagram comparing life in the city and country.

❑ Contact train, bus, and airlines for round trip fares to big cities near you. Have students compare the price and amount of time required for each trip. Which means of transportation is the best? Why?

❑ Have students use a map to plot a trip from their hometown to a big city nearby. List highway numbers and landmarks, and calculate mileage if possible.

❑ Have students look at the map to locate a big city to the north, south, east, and west. Do research to learn about places to visit in each city. Make a graph showing which city your students would prefer to visit.

❑ With the class, make a graph of the different car makes owned by the families in your class.

Creative Writing Questions and Topics

❑ Keep a journal telling details about a car trip with your family.

❑ Write about the last movie or the last restaurant meal on the trip.

❑ Interview the person in your family who will prepare the family car for a trip. What must that person do?

Bibliography

Dear Brother by Frank Asch (Scholastic Books, 1991)

City/Country by Ken Robbins (Viking Press, 1985)

Across Town by Sara (Orchard Books, 1991)

Clockwork

Activity Sheet 1: Here are some important events from the story. Set the clocks to tell what time they may have occurred.

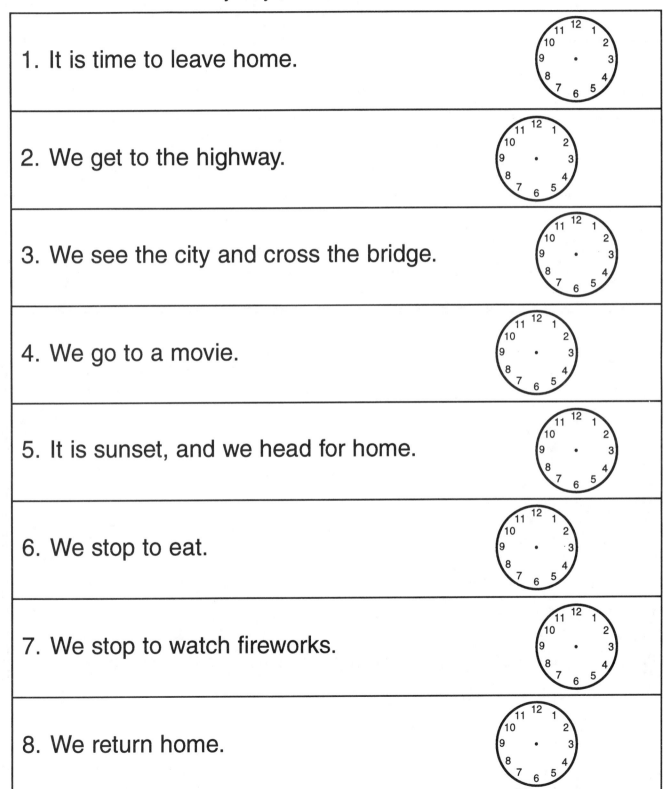

1. It is time to leave home.

2. We get to the highway.

3. We see the city and cross the bridge.

4. We go to a movie.

5. It is sunset, and we head for home.

6. We stop to eat.

7. We stop to watch fireworks.

8. We return home.

A Story and a Picture

Activity Sheet 2: Use this page to write a story about the place where you live. Draw a picture of an important place in your town or city.

_____

_____

_____

_____

_____

_____

The Thirteenth Clue

Summary

A young girl follows thirteen clues to a surprise birthday party.

Activities

❑ The clues in this book are given in a variety of ways. Children will enjoy writing their names or brief messages in the following ways:

- with yarn or string and glue on paper
- with toothpicks glued to paper
- in sand or clay
- with small pebbles on the floor or table
- with letter cubes from a Boggle game

❑ Have the students write a sequel to this book, telling about the birthday party.

❑ Have students work in groups to hide an object in the room and write a set of clues to help another group locate it.

❑ Plan a surprise party. Include games, refreshments, and decorations. If possible, have a small party as a culminating activity.

❑ Make construction paper balloons to use for a variety of math activities. You will need 26 balloons of different colors to prepare concentration-style matching games for numerals (1–13) and number words, or numbers and sets. Students may choose a numeral, turn the other balloons to the blank side, and count sets. Use the numeral balloons for identifying ordinal numbers, putting a group of items in consecutive order, or sequencing a group of random numbers.

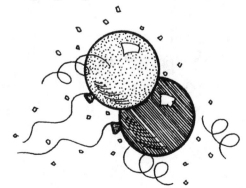

The Thirteenth Clue (cont.)

Activities (cont.)

❑ Some of the clues were given as scrambled words. Unscramble the birthday vocabulary in the activity sheet on page 89.

❑ With the class, rewrite the text of this book in standard sentences.

❑ Encourage the students to write and decode secret messages.

❑ Provide samples of backward printing. Decode it by looking in a mirror. Have students choose a partner and stand facing each other. They should pretend they are looking in a mirror and copy each other's movements.

❑ Discuss what diaries are and why some people write in them. Encourage your students to keep a diary (journal) for a week.

❑ Have the students draw the text of the book into a large poster (map), beginning at the girl's house and ending at the party in the woods.

❑ Using a Venn diagram, have students compare and contrast this book with *The Secret Birthday Message* by Eric Carle, Harper and Row, 1971.

Creative Writing Questions and Topics:

❑ How would you feel if your birthday was forgotten?

❑ What is in your attic?

❑ Do you enjoy surprises? Why? Why not?

❑ Have you ever had a surprise party? Tell about one you know of.

Bibliography

Night Noises by Mem Fox (Harcourt, 1989)

The Birthday Door by Eve Merriam (Morrow, 1986)

Nate the Great and the Snowy Trail by Marjorie Sharmat (Dell, 1984)

Surprise! Surprise! by Molly Mia Stewart (Bantam, 1989)

Scrambled Words

Activity Sheet 1: Unscramble the birthday vocabulary words.

1. BLOLASNO   _____

2. SRPIESUR   _____

3. PYTAR   _____

4. SAMEG   _____

5. AKCE   _____

6. THYADRIB   _____

7. CLEADN   _____

8. CCEIERAM   _____

ice cream	candle
birthday	cake
games	party
surprise	balloons

Mystery Message

Activity Sheet 2: Read the 13 clues below and decode this message. Fill in each blank with the correct letter. Copy each new letter in the properly numbered balloons and color them.

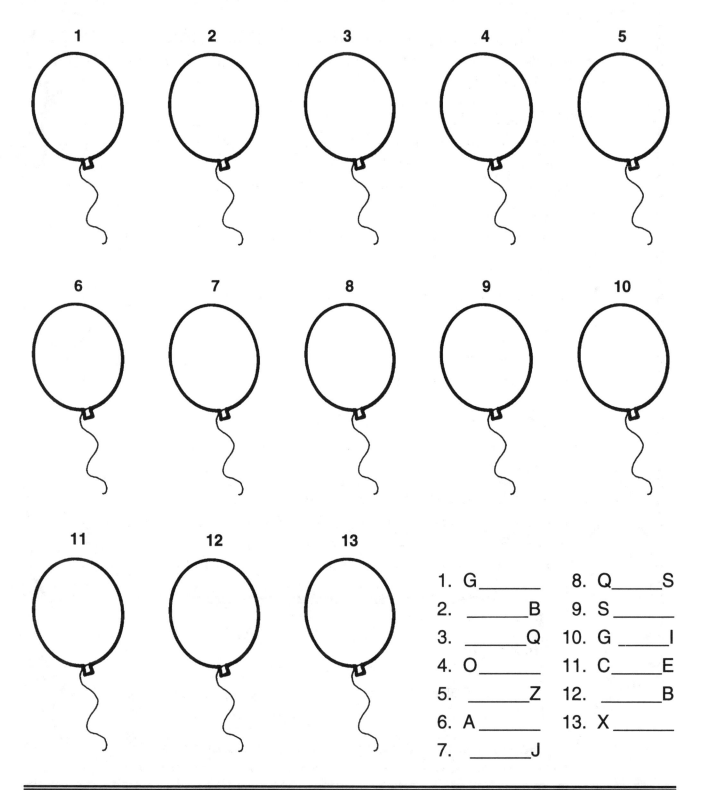

1. G_____   8. Q_____S
2. _____B   9. S_____
3. _____Q   10. G ____I
4. O_____   11. C_____E
5. _____Z   12. _____B
6. A_____   13. X_____
7. _____J

The Trek

Summary

A young girl imagines that she passes a variety of jungle animals as she walks to school. The reader becomes involved in her visual game of hidden pictures in the scenes along the way.

Activities

- ❏ Before beginning the book, discuss the meaning of the word *trek*. Ask the children where they usually go when they take a walk.

- ❏ Make a graph of the class showing which students walk or ride to school.

- ❏ Have the students find the animals hidden in the activity sheet on page 92.

- ❏ Have the students make a list of the animals hidden in the story. (Check the back of the book for information.) Classify the animals into jungle or desert habitats.

- ❏ Be sure to look at the clouds in each picture. Ask the students what they can find.

- ❏ Share some other popular books that feature hidden pictures, like the *I Spy* and *Waldo* books.

- ❏ Help children make a map of their walk to school. Write a story about anything unusual they might have seen along the way.

- ❏ Research facts about one (or all) of the animals pictured in the book.

- ❏ Have children draw or trace animals and create their own hidden pictures by adding scenery around them.

Creative Writing Questions and Topics

- ❏ What do you see on your way to school? What is the most interesting thing that you see?

- ❏ How would the story have been different if the animals had been real?

- ❏ Do you enjoy books that include a visual game? Why? Why not?

- ❏ What do you think the girl told her classmates when she got to the room?

Bibliography

Junglewalk by Nancy Tafuri (Greenwillow Books, 1988)

I Can Take a Walk by Shigeo Watanabe (Putnam, 1984)

Find Five

Activity Sheet 1: Find five animals hidden in this picture.

Two Bear Cubs

Summary

Two bear cubs share a day-long adventure as they begin to gain independence from their mother's watchful eye.

Activities

- ❏ As you read the story, have the children look for the mother bear in each picture.
- ❏ This book is done in green, blue, and brown. Have children select three different colors and write and illustrate a similar story using different animals.
- ❏ Have students write an innovation (or adaptation of this story) using two children and their mother in place of the bears.
- ❏ Have students write (or dictate) the story from the point of view of one of the cubs.
- ❏ Have students make a list of the events in the cubs' day and a child's typical (weekend) day. Compare and contrast the two. Was the mother always present for both?
- ❏ Brainstorm a list of adjectives to describe the bear cubs: *curious, lost, playful, hungry,* etc. How can those words also be used to describe children?
- ❏ Have students fill in the pictures to complete the story map on page 94.
- ❏ Have the class research information about hibernation. List five facts that pertain to brown bears. Make a diorama to illustrate hibernation.
- ❏ Research facts about brown bears. Have the students answer these questions: What do they eat? How big are they? Make a drawing of their footprints and locate their habitats on a U.S. map.
- ❏ Have students compare and contrast the life of a bear in the wild and in the zoo.
- ❏ Laminate sheets of several colors of construction paper. Cut out small bear shapes to use in patterning, sorting, or counting activities.
- ❏ Make the bear on page 95. You will need scissors, crayons, and three paper fasteners for each student. If you wish, you may enlarge the patterns to make a mother bear.

Creative Writing Questions and Topics

- ❏ How would you feel if you went somewhere and became lost from your mother? What would you do?
- ❏ What kinds of things can you do without going far from your home?

Bibliography

How Do Bears Sleep? by E. J. Bird (Carolrhoda Books, 1990)

Good Morning, Baby Bear by Eric Hill (Random House, 1984)

Where's the Bear? by Charlotte Pomerantz (Greenwillow Books, 1984)

Make a Map

Activity Sheet 1: Read the words and add the pictures to complete the story map.

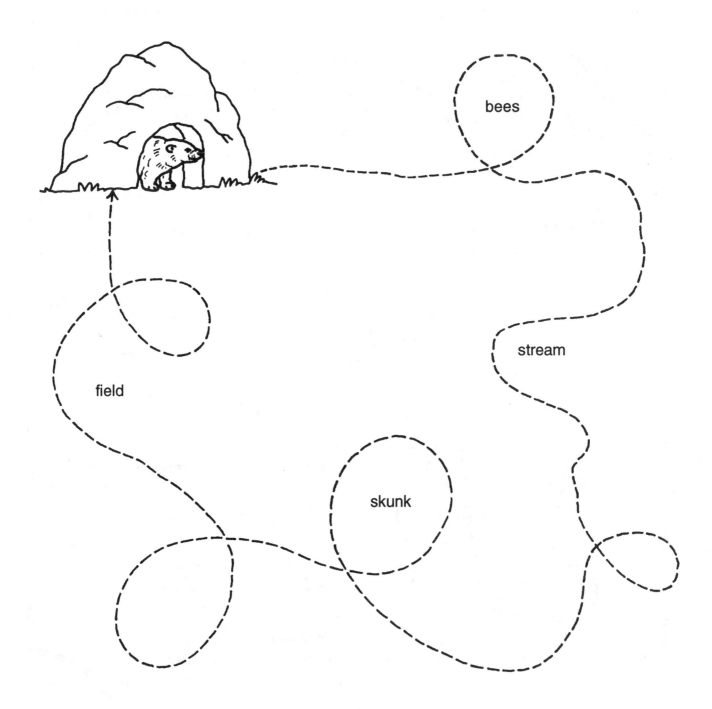

Build a Bear

Activity Sheet 2: Color and cut out the pieces to make a bear. Join the legs and head with paper fasteners.

When You Were a Baby

Summary

In her first book, Ann Jonas pictures a variety of things that babies cannot do. At the end of the book, she points out that those things become easy once the child has grown.

Activities

❑ After you share this book, ask children to suggest a list of other things that babies cannot do.

❑ Ask the students to describe objects in the book without looking back at the pictures (boat, bear, doll, etc.).

❑ Point out the author's use of patterns (stripes and blocks). Look for similar patterns in your environment and picture them.

❑ Provide a set of small wooden blocks with letters. Students may use these to spell their names or words from the book. You may also prepare the blocks as scrambled words to be used with a word list.

❑ Ask children to work in groups to draw a time line showing growth from baby to adult. If appropriate, they may assign ages to the pictures and write sentences about different life stages.

❑ Have students make small personal books with blue or pink covers, telling about themselves as babies or telling about a baby sibling.

❑ Ask students to bring in baby pictures of themselves to share. Display them on a bulletin board titled "When We Were Babies." You may wish to display the pictures without names and have students guess to whom they belong. Number the pictures and provide a numbered key.

❑ If possible, set up a center for pouring, measuring, and mixing. You will need several scoops, buckets, and containers of various sizes. Children will enjoy pouring and measuring rice, beans, or sand. If you have a water table, they may mix sand and water to make a sand castle as pictured in the book.

❑ Share the following poems from *The Random House Book of Poetry for Children* (1983): "Did You?" by William Cole, "Six Weeks Old" by Christopher Morley, "Some Things Don't Make Any Sense at All" by Judith Viorst, and "Misnomer" by Eve Merriam. All these poems focus on events in a baby's life.

Creative Writing Questions and Topics

❑ What are some things that babies can do?

❑ Do you ever wish you were still a baby? Why?

❑ What is your earliest memory? What were you doing?

Bibliography

The New Baby at Your House by Joanna Cole (William Morrow, 1985)

On the Day You Were Born by Debra Frasier (HBJ, 19910

When I Was Little by Lyn Littlefield Hooper (Dutton, 1983)

Babies! by Dorothy Hinshaw Patent (Holiday House, 1988)

Past, Present, Future

Activity Sheet 1: Complete this chart with information about your life before, now, and in the future.

	Baby	Now	Adult
Food			
Work			
Play			
Clothing			

Activity Sheet 2: Complete the birth certificate with facts about your birth. At the bottom, draw some toys that you think a baby would like.

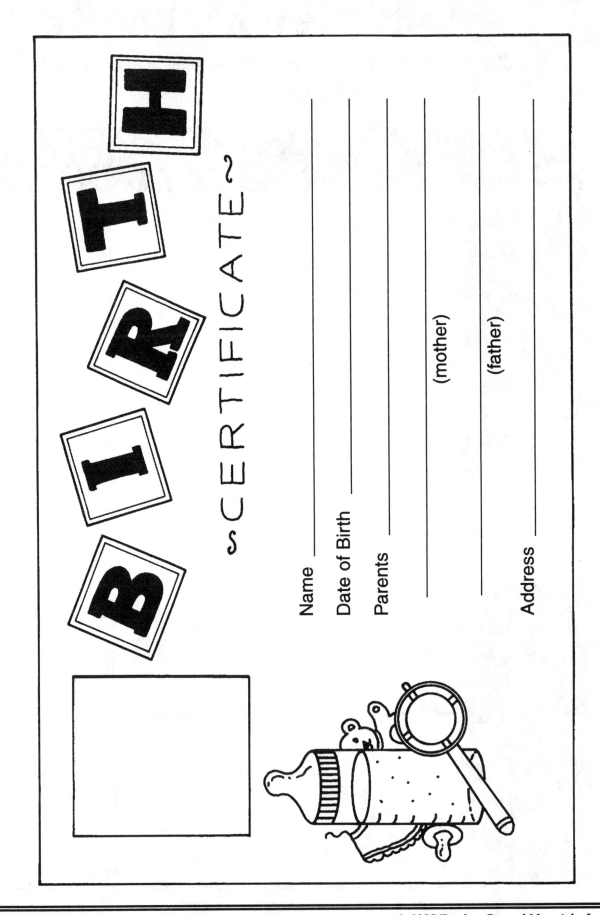

BIRTH CERTIFICATE

Name _____

Date of Birth _____

Parents _____
(mother)

_____
(father)

Address _____

Where Can It Be?

Summary

A little girl searches everywhere for her lost blanket which is finally returned by her friend Deborah.

Activities

❑ Make a flap book showing five places that things get lost at your house. Think about the kinds of things that grown-ups often misplace (keys, glasses, etc.).

❑ Visit your school lost-and-found room. Ask students whether there is anything that belongs to them or someone they know. What can be done with the unclaimed items?

❑ Have students make a reward poster for something that is lost (like a pet). Include a picture and description, where the item was last seen, where to call if you have information, and the reward if appropriate.

❑ Play simple hiding games like the following:

   • Hide 100 pennies around the room. Give students a limited amount of time to locate them.

   • Have students locate a common item, using verbal or written clues from class members.

   • Hide an item in plain sight. Instruct students to search until they find it and then sit down without giving away the location. The last student seated will hide the item in the next round.

❑ Brainstorm a list of things in the classroom (or at home) that can be opened—boxes, doors, jars, etc.

❑ Have students make a posters of their bedrooms or kitchens. Each poster should have at least three flaps to lift.

❑ Use nouns pictured in the book to reinforce initial consonants:
-lanket, -oys, -ress, -ook (**b**lanket, **t**oys, **d**ress, **b**ook)

Creative Writing Questions and Topics

❑ What is the worst thing you could lose?

❑ Did/do you have a favorite blanket? Describe it and tell why it is special.

❑ How would the little girl have felt if she had never found her blanket? What could she have done?

Bibliography

Moongame by Frank Asch (Prentice-Hall, 1984)

Where Is Mittens? by Kelly Boivin (Children's Press, 1990)

Where Is the Bear? by Bonnie Larkin Nims (A. Whitman, 1988)

Fill Them Full!

Activity Sheet 1: Take this sheet home and draw things that are in your clothes closet and refrigerator. Cut out the doors and glue them in place.

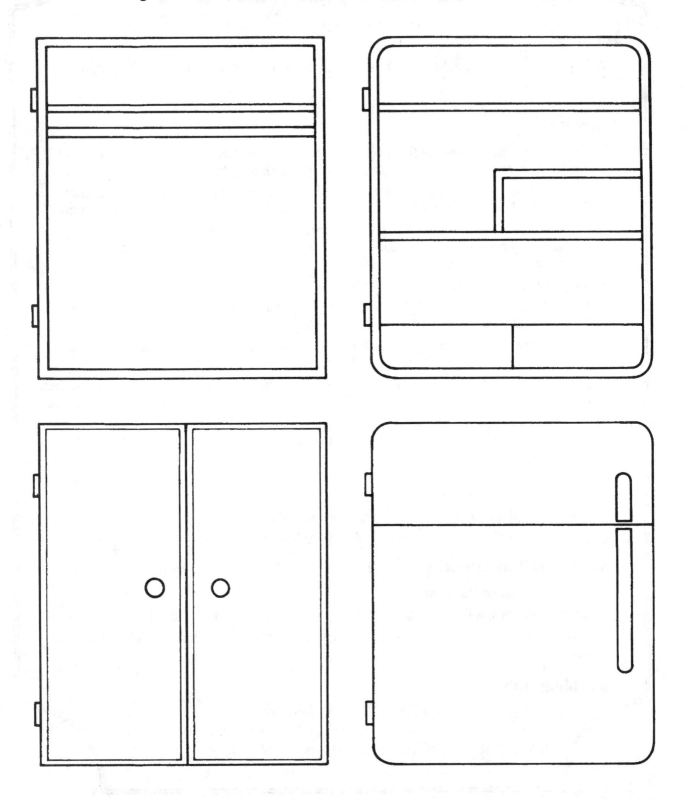

Search Sequence

Activity Sheet 2: Put a number in each blank box to show the order in which the little girl searched her house. Complete the pictures.

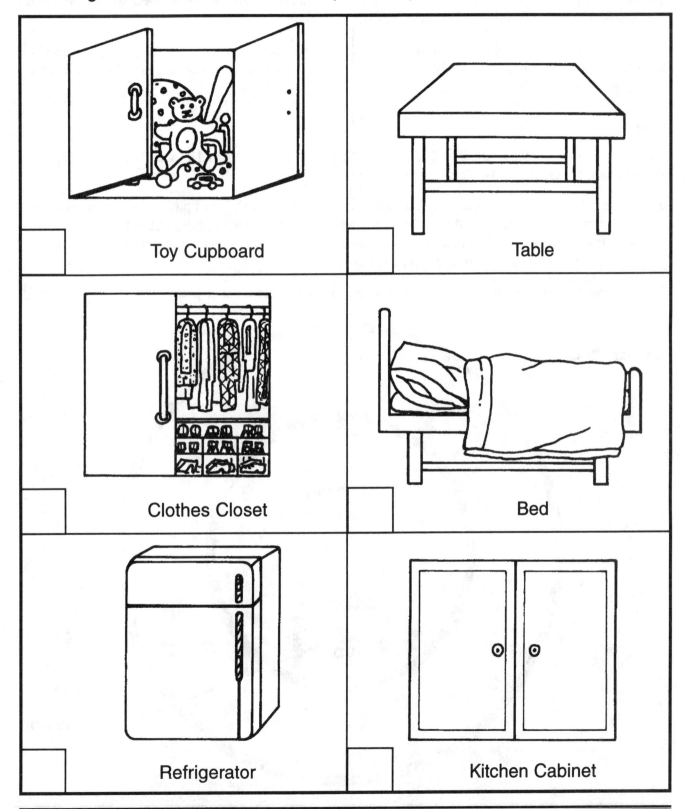

Toy Cupboard

Table

Clothes Closet

Bed

Refrigerator

Kitchen Cabinet

Theme Parade

Your students will enjoy making hats and vests for a Donald Crews/Ann Jonas theme parade. They may choose to share the costumes and student-made books from this unit with others through an actual parade or by inviting guests (another class or family members) to visit and hear their stories. When the activity is finished, consider featuring the items in a display.

To get started, post a list of titles and discuss symbols that would be appropriate for decorating the hats and vests. Some patterns that will help you are on pages 103–105; others are located throughout this book. Have each student choose his favorite book to use as a theme.

Hat

Materials: the hat pattern on page 103, desired clip art, several colors of 18" x 24" (46 cm x 60 cm) construction paper, glue, tape, scissors, and markers

Directions: Design the crown of your hat on a 6" x 21" (15 cm x 52.5 cm) piece of construction paper. Form the strip into a cylinder and tape the short ends together. Do not overlap the paper. Trace and cut the brim from a 12" x 12" (30 cm x 30 cm) piece of paper. Cut out the center carefully (page 103). Fold the tabs up and glue or tape the brim in place.

For variety, students may make simple crowns, visors, or hats from paper plates.

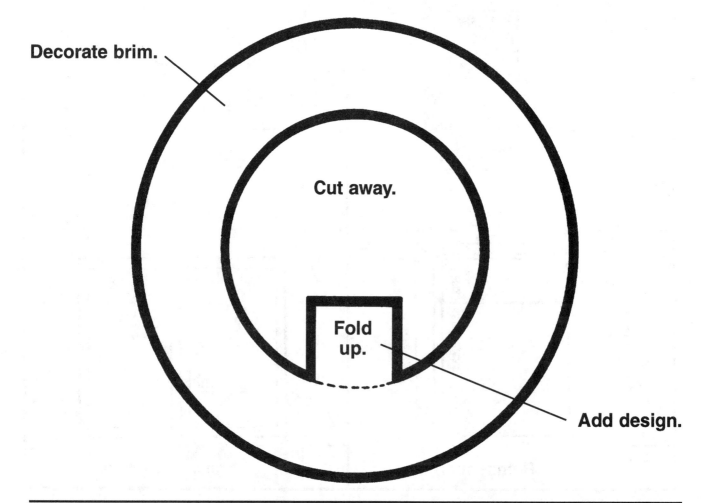

Decorate brim.

Cut away.

Fold up.

Add design.

Theme Parade *(cont.)*

Hat Brim

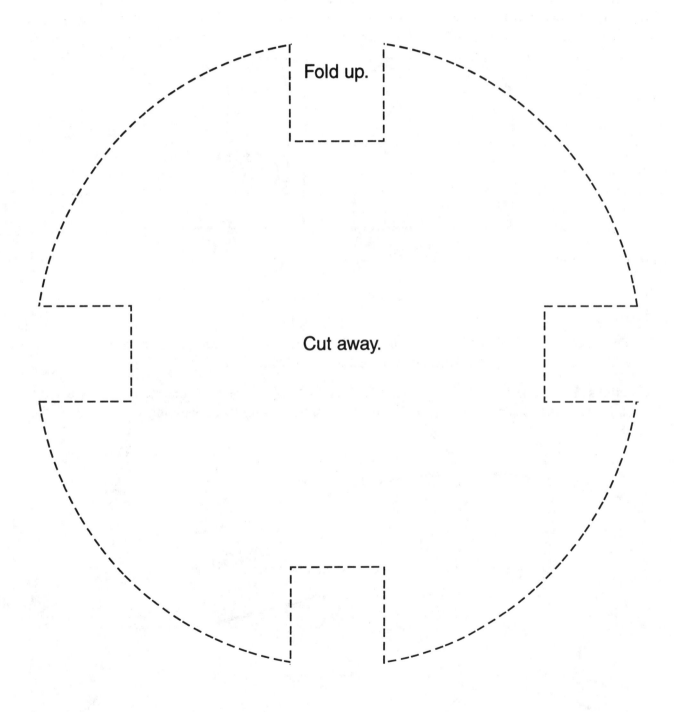

Fold up.

Cut away.

Theme Parade *(cont.)*

Vest

Materials: brown paper grocery bag, scissors, markers or crayons, glue, scrap construction paper

Directions: Push out the sides of the bag and lay it flat. Cut the armholes and neck as shown. Cut open the front. Carefully turn the bag inside out so that no print will be showing.

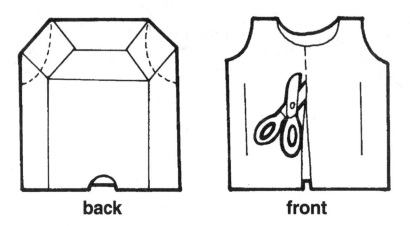

back   **front**

Banners

Materials: two long cardboard tubes (from wrapping paper) a long piece of white paper about 12" x 48" (30 cm x 122 cm), markers or crayons, glue, and tape

Directions: Design banners showing the authors' names and/or book titles on the paper. Glue and tape the ends securely to the cardboard tubes. Have two students carry them, walking side by side in the parade.

Theme Parade (cont.)

Assessment Activities

Knowledge: This level of assessment provides students with an opportunity to recall fundamental facts and information about the story.

Here are a few ideas you can adapt to any of the books you have read with your students.

❑ Make a story map showing the sequence of events and/or locations in the story. Begin by deciding what events you will include. Make a series of small pictures to represent them. Join the pictures with arrows to make a path from beginning to end. You may number the pictures in order and use the story map to retell the story to another class.

❑ Make a matching game of pictures and labels for vocabulary practice.

❑ Print the book title on tagboard and cut apart the letters. Store several titles in separate envelopes. Students will organize the letters for spelling practice.

❑ Ask students to create a word search puzzle with vocabulary from the story.

❑ If appropriate, prepare cards with terms and definitions from the book. Separate the term from the definition for a matching activity.

❑ Prepare sentence cards for main ideas or events in the book. Students will read the cards and arrange them in consecutive order.

Comprehension: This level of assessment provides students with an opportunity to demonstrate a basic understanding of the story.

❑ Complete the web diagram on page 107 with information about a specific book.

❑ Prepare several pictures for each of the titles you have used in class. Use them for a game in which the student looks at a picture and responds with the related book title.

❑ Use the form on page 108 to design a game board for one or several titles. The students will write true/false or comprehension questions.

❑ Have each student write a 20-question "test" about one or several books. Class members will trade the papers and answer the questions.

❑ Students may write and share riddles about terms they have learned from the book(s).

Assessment Activities *(cont.)*

Comprehension: Complete this web diagram with information from the book.

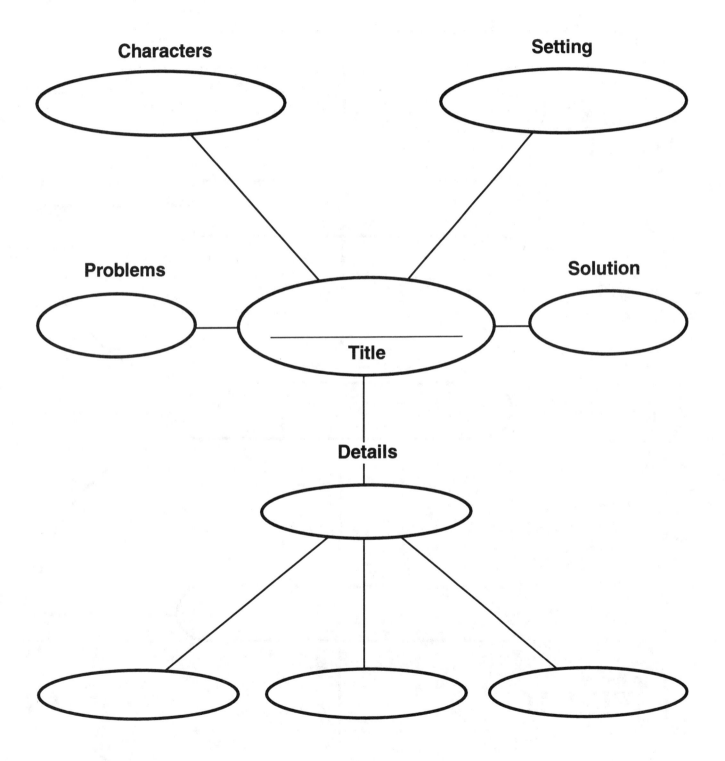

Assessment Activities *(cont.)*

Comprehension *(cont.):* Design a game board for our book. Remember to write questions for your game.

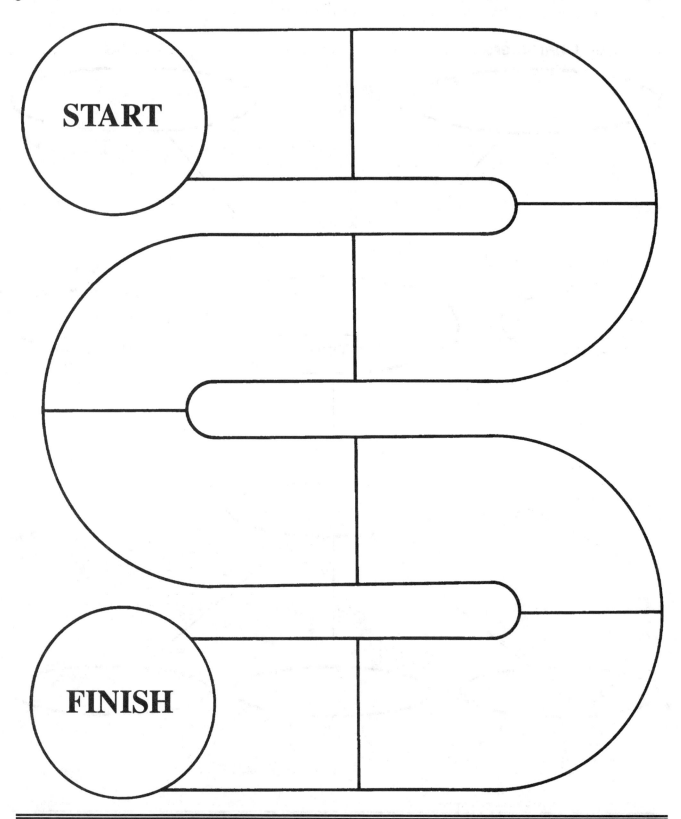

Assessment Activities *(cont.)*

Application: This level of assessment provides students with an opportunity to use information about or from the story in a new way.

- ❑ Provide a variety of art supplies for students to make a diorama about the theme of the book.

- ❑ Assign names to the people pictured in the book(s). Rewrite a scene from the book as fiction with a group of characters.

- ❑ Fill in the words on the activity sheet on page 110 and distribute.

- ❑ Students should illustrate the words, cut apart the pages, and staple them together in alphabetical order. Use this for a spelling resource for creative writing.

- ❑ Design a book jacket or bookmark related to the theme of the book. Display the book jackets on a bulletin board. Use the bookmarks for personal reading.

- ❑ Use the encyclopedia to do additional research about one of the themes that interests you. Write and illustrate five new facts that you learned. Use these pages to write a sequel to your book.

- ❑ Read another book by the same author. Prepare a "lesson plan" with three activities to share with the class.

Assessment Activities *(cont.)*

Application: Use this form to make a mini-dictionary with vocabulary from your book. Cut apart the pages and staple them into a book in ABC order.

Assessment Activities *(cont.)*

Analysis: This level of assessment provides your students with an opportunity to examine a part of the story or the style of the author carefully in order to better understand it.

- ❑ Have students write a letter to the author (see page 112), telling about their favorite book and asking questions about the author's style of writing. Why is the theme important to the author and children?

- ❑ Use a Venn diagram to compare and contrast the illustrating and writing styles of this author with another author of your choice.

Synthesis: This level of assessment provides students with an opportunity to put parts from the story together in a new way to form a new idea or product.

- ❑ Ask students to think of themselves as a character in the book. They should write a personal scene using the subject of the book as a setting.

- ❑ Rewrite the story from a different point of view . . . a fly on the wall, a pet, or a narrator.

- ❑ Choose a different nonfiction subject that interests you. Research the subject. Organize the information into a new book with similar format and art.

- ❑ Prepare word wheels using vocabulary from the book. There should be one wheel for each different part of speech—nouns, verbs, and adjectives. The student will spin and write (or speak) sentences that include the indicated words. If appropriate, the students may illustrate the sentences and combine them into books with several of their friends.

- ❑ List three "splinter" (related) topics for one of the books. Choose one topic to research. Write five statements with information about the new topic.

Evaluation: This level of assessment provides the students with an opportunity to form and present an opinion backed up by sound reasoning.

- ❑ Choose the book you liked the best. Prepare a speech recommending it to others. Listen to several speeches. Follow with a poll of the class to determine who was the most persuasive.

- ❑ Compare two books by this author. Discuss how they are alike and different.

- ❑ How would your life be different without the subject or concept of this book? Discuss with other class members. Record your opinions and share with the class.

Assessment Activities *(cont.)*

Analysis: Use this stationery to write a letter to the author.